AMERICAN POETS PROJECT

AMERICAN POETS PROJECT

IS PUBLISHED WITH A GIFT IN MEMORY OF

James Merrill

AND SUPPORT FROM ITS FOUNDING PATRONS

Sidney J. Weinberg, Jr. Foundation

The Berkley Foundation

Richard B. Fisher and Jeanne Donovan Fisher

Ira Gershwin

SELECTED LYRICS —

EDITED BY
ROBERT KIMBALL

WITHDRAWN

AMERICAN POETS PROJECT

THE LIBRARY OF AMERICA

Special thanks to Michael S. Strunsky and Michael Owen.

Introduction, volume compilation, and notes copyright © 2009 by Literary Classics of the United States, Inc. All rights reserved. Printed in the United States of America. No part of this book may be reproduced in any manner whatsoever without permission.

Lyrics used by permission of Ira and Leonore Gershwin Trusts, Michael S. Strunsky, Trustee. See page 160 for copyrights and acknowledgments.

The paper used in this publication meets the minimum requirements of the American National Standard for Information Sciences—Permanence of Paper for Printed Library Materials, ANSI Z39.48—1984.

Design by Chip Kidd and Mark Melnick.
Photo facing Contents courtesy of the Ira and Leonore Gershwin Trusts.

Library of Congress Control Number: 2009929599
ISBN 978-1-59853-052-1
American Poets Project—29

First Printing

Ira Gershwin

CONTENTS

INTRODUCTION

Ira Gershwin mused often about lyrics and the process of writing them. This humorous account—never before published—of "how the lyrics [of a show or film] are written" was jotted down on three undated yellow legal-pad pages:

You work all afternoon with the composer. He either (A) has a tune ready for you which you may or may not like, or (B) is struggling with one. Or (C) you both sit around dolefully until he gets one or at least a start on one.

If A—and you like—you try to get a title or some lines which may lead to a title (you already know what the situation called for, whether it is for a solo, duet, trio; if the mood is to be joyous, melancholy). Sometimes you have an inevitable title and a couple of lines which he likes. In either instance you struggle for hours and finally something is fairly well set (which next day you may or may not throw out). If there is no meeting of the minds as regards melody or words you both sit around and commiserate and say, "This sure is a tough way to make a living." If the composer can't stay for dinner there are probably other guests. After 3 or 4 hours of discussing whatever the guests or you are interested in, or playing Scrabble, or listening to radio, or watching TV or whatever, around midnight you excuse yourself politely. So to your workroom, to rework the afternoon's work or to see if you can get any ideas for other numbers that have to be written.

You are now alone & of course have to see what's in the evening papers, read several magazines you're behind on, look up Fowler on some particular usage which usually you don't get to because on the 1st page you've opened to there is a delectable discussion of some other usage you've forgotten about & something Fowler says leads to other books of reference—or the Britannica or one of the 24 volumes of the Dict. of Nat. Biography and suddenly you remember you didn't get a chance at noon's coffee to go thru all the mail and that has to be taken care of and it's now 3 a.m. and the house is quiet and you go down to the kitchen and make yourself a couple of sandwiches downed with milk or root beer then back to work and you work for 2 or 3 hours until it's pretty light outside and finally at 6 a.m. you get to bed, take a sleeping pill—but you're so stimulated by what you've done that you like or so depressed by what you didn't like—that you know the pill won't work for an hour or two—and you get hold of some more magazines or the latest novel or again Fowler or a book of light verse or "Punchiana" (London 1850) or the closing market quotations or if it is early Sat. morning in season you go out on the lawn to get the morning paper

for the sport pages to see what names you can con-
jure up to be on at the races and if you're lucky
you're asleep by 7 or 7:30 a.m. and the alarm clock
wakes you at 12 and you dress, shave, have coffee &
a Dexedrine and on weekdays you go thru the same
afternoon's business, but if Sat. in season you're off
to the track (doctor's orders so you get some exer-
cise). And that's how lyrics are written.

In the early 1970s, when I was interviewing Ira for *The
Gershwins*, a pictorial biography I wrote with Alfred
Simon, he described in a more serious vein how he and his
brother, George, his principal collaborator, approached
songs. "We worked best under deadlines and we worked
mostly at night," he recalled. "Before getting to work we
would go to the kitchen and have ice cream and figure out
what we had to do. George's mind and his notebooks were
full of tunes. There were times when his melodies would
pour out so quickly and naturally that he would have sev-
eral ideas in a day. Usually, if we were happy with some-
thing he had written, I would memorize it and try to find a
title or idea for it. The title and the last line of the refrain
were most important to me."

"Good lyrics," Ira told George's early biographer,
Isaac Goldberg, "should be simple, colloquial, rhymed
conversation." He once said to me that he always tried to
"capture the way people spoke to each other—their slang,
their clichés, the catchphrases."

Ira Gershwin wrote lyrics at a time when songs were
looked upon as goods and merchandise, products to be
pushed and peddled in vaudeville houses and five-and-ten-
cent stores, in sheet music form or on recordings. But the
songs, once considered as obsolescent as last year's fash-
ions, turned out to be among the most enduring artistic

expressions of their times. I remember a summer afternoon in 1972 when Ira was singing for me the exquisite verse of his song "Delishious" and telling me that the title of his little-known "Gather Ye Rosebuds" was derived from a line of a poem by Robert Herrick. The phone rang. It was Ira's friend Oscar Levant calling to urge Ira to turn on Mike Douglas's television show: there was Benny Goodman playing "Oh, Lady, Be Good!" on his clarinet. It was a song that had been evoked over the years by such diverse authors as John Galsworthy in his 1926 play *Escape* and by Ezra Pound in his "Canto LXXIV." When Goodman finished, Ira said, "George and I wrote that song in 1924. I can't believe it's still being played today."

Ira Gershwin was born December 6, 1896, in a building on the corner of Hester and Eldridge streets on the Lower East Side of Manhattan. He recalled that before he was 20 years old his family, which consisted of his parents, his younger brothers George and Arthur, and his sister, Frances, had lived in 28 different places. In many ways this peripatetic early life helped make him a reader. "I kept clippings of columns by F.P.A. (Franklin Pierce Adams), C. L. Edson, and others and immersed myself in books," he remembered. By 1912 he was devouring more than a book a week; by the end of his life he owned and had read thousands of books. A look at his library revealed books by George Ade, Max Beerbohm, Robert Benchley, Arnold Bennett, W. S. Gilbert, O. Henry, Ring Lardner, A. J. Liebling, Don Marquis, Somerset Maugham, H. L. Mencken, Ogden Nash, George Jean Nathan, Dorothy Parker, S. J. Perelman, H. G. Wells, his close friend P. G. Wodehouse, many biographies and countless reference works, dictionaries, and other indispensables such as Bartlett, Bullfinch, Fowler, and Roget.

Ira also loved the theater, frequently attending revues and extravaganzas as a young man. He especially cherished the Guy Bolton–P. G. Wodehouse–Jerome Kern "Princess Theatre" shows, noted for their suave melodies and urbane lyrics. He was fond of quoting Wodehouse lyrics, taking particular delight in the couplet "Whenever he dances / His partner takes chances," from the earliest version of the song "Bill," written for the 1918 show *Oh, Lady! Lady!*

Significantly, it was George and Ira Gershwin who inherited the mantle of the "Princess" collaborators. Starting in 1924 with *Lady, Be Good!*, the brothers succeeded in creating a series of lighthearted, smart shows that captured much of the infectious spirit of the Princess offerings. For instance, in the song "'S Wonderful" (*Funny Face*, 1927), Ira's ingenious use of fused syllables (*'S wonderful, 'S paradise, 'S marvelous*) and clipped syllables (*pash, fash, emosh, devosh*) masterfully conveyed an effervescence that his biographer Philip Furia described as "the giddiness of romantic union." In his book *Lyrics on Several Occasions*, Ira commented that his main goal in this lyric "was to feature the sibilant sound effect by deleting the 'it' of 'it's' and slurring the leftover 's' with the first syllable of the following word. So I'm completely baffled by what some singers have in mind and throat when they formalize the phrases to '*It's* wonderful,' '*It's* marvelous' . . ." Ira first employed the clipping of syllables, one of his favorite devices, in the 1926 song "Sunny Disposish," which he wrote with composer Philip Charig for *Americana*. In *Lyrics on Several Occasions*, he noted that he got the idea after hearing comedian Walter Catlett clipping syllables in *Lady, Be Good!*

The Gershwins also excelled in high voltage rhythm songs. The challenging musical complexities of "Fascinating Rhythm," "Sweet and Low-Down," "My One and Only," and "I Got Rhythm" elicited virtuosic lyrics from

Ira that pulsated in their own right. Interestingly, the original title of "Fascinating Rhythm" was "Syncopated City." Ira would return to that riveting evocation of the city in his little-known "New York Serenade" ("Ten thousand steamboats hootin' / A million taxis tootin'"), the 1940's revised lyric of "Fascinating Rhythm," and the 1949 "Manhattan Downbeat."

What many believe to be George and Ira's finest work was realized during the year between the summers of 1936 and 1937 when they were in Hollywood writing for the movies, a period that produced such gems as "They Can't Take That Away From Me," "Nice Work If You Can Get It," and "Love Is Here to Stay." Tragically, George died in July 1937 at age 38 of a brain tumor. "No one," their friend and colleague Irving Berlin said to me during one of our occasional phone conversations, "wrote greater songs than George and Ira did during the last year of George's life." Berlin then sang for me "A Foggy Day," proclaiming it "perfect" and admonishing me, "Never forget how great Ira was." I haven't.

Ira had many successes after George's death, including the show *Lady in the Dark* (1941) and such songs as "I Can't Get Started," "Long Ago (and Far Away)," and "The Man That Got Away," but he never recovered fully from the loss of his brother. His career effectively ended in the mid-1950s. He died in 1983 in his longtime home in Beverly Hills, California; he was 86 years old.

While not a substitute for Ira's own classic of 50 years ago, *Lyrics on Several Occasions*, with 104 lyrics (one more, he told me, than a compilation of 103 Cole Porter lyrics) annotated and arranged topically, or *The Complete Lyrics of Ira Gershwin*, a compendium of more than 700 lyrics which I edited in 1993, the present volume does aim to provide a compact distillation of Ira's lyric genius. The lyrics presented here in chronological order—some well known, others not, without commentary or reference to their show or movie sources—are those that can stand best on their own as verse. They range from his first published lyric, "You May Throw All the Rice You Desire," written in 1917, to some of his brilliant songs for the 1954 film *A Star Is Born*. Since this is a collection spotlighting the work of Ira Gershwin, I have not included any of the lyrics he collaborated on with other lyricists.

Here, then, is the essential Ira, with all his wit, romance, and dazzling virtuosity.

Robert Kimball

You May Throw All the Rice You Desire

The ceremony was over,
And all was happy and gay.
The blushing bride and her lover
To the steps did wend their way.
Their young friends them had preceded
And had formed a merry plot;
Although the older folks pleaded,
The younger folks heeded them not.
But the bridegroom knew all about it,
And he stood with his haughty head,
He lifted his hand (you may doubt it,
But 'tis true), these words he said:

REFRAIN
"You may throw all the rice you desire,
But please, friends, throw no shoes.
For 'twill surely arouse my ire,
If you cause my wife one bruise.
Should you heed these words and don't fire,
Then my friendship you won't lose.
You may throw all the rice you desire,
But please, friends, throw no shoes."

VERSE 2
A thrill o'er that throng so motley
Went like a flash so quick;
And many young faces flamed hotly,
Their consciences made them sick.

Many a spirit so reckless
Was beginning to meditate.
Persons with souls not so fleckess
Their wrongdoings vowed to abate.
As the decades rolled by, they never
Forgot that brave husband's part.
They behaved thereafter, forever,
Like they knew, as follows, by heart:

REPEAT REFRAIN

The Real American Folk Song
(Is a Rag)

VERSE I
Near Barcelona the peasant croons
The old traditional Spanish tunes;
The Neapolitan Street Song sighs—
You think of Italian skies.
Each nation has a creative vein
Originating a native strain,
With folk songs plaintive and others gay
In their own peculiar way.
American folk songs, I feel,
Have a much stronger appeal.

The real American folk song is a rag—
A mental jag—
A rhythmic tonic for the chronic blues.
The critics called it a joke song, but now
They've changed their tune
And they like it somehow.
For it's inoculated
With a syncopated
Sort of meter,
Sweeter
Than a classic strain;
Boy! You can't remain
Still and quiet—
For it's a riot!
The real American folk song
Is like a Fountain of Youth:
You taste, and it elates you,
And then invigorates you.
The real American folk song—
A masterstroke song—
IS A RAG!

VERSE 2

You may dislike or you may adore
The native songs from a foreign shore;
They may be songs that you can't forget,
They may be distinctive, yet—
They lack a something: a certain snap,
The tempo ticklish that makes you tap,
The invitation to agitate—

And leave the rest to Fate.
A raggy refrain anytime
Sends me a message sublime.

REPEAT REFRAIN

I'm Tickled Silly

VERSE
When the lastest film by Sennett
Or by Fox is mentioned, then it
Is my one and burning wish
To get a seat for it.
All the highbrows call 'em frightful,
But for my part they're delightful,
So I comb the town and look
On ev'ry street for it.
I'm a gent, and I'm a scholar,
Yet I'd part with my last dollar
Just to see a slapstick artist frolic.
Though there's nothing that's dramatic
In his actions acrobatic,
There's an end to all that's melancholic.

REFRAIN I
I'm tickled silly
When there is a scene
Where a chap gets a rap
On the bean;

When, willy-nilly,
A brick or a pie
Comes to rest on his chest
Or his eye.
Life is complete
When I gaze at his feet
As they gambol all over the street.
Off goes a gun,
And I chortle with glee,
When, on the run,
They all fall in the sea.
I laugh when they soak 'em,
I roar when they choke 'em,
The old movie hokum for me.

VERSE 2

When you see a film by Chaplin,
Though your name be Smith or Kaplan,
I am very sure you're bound to be hilarious;
With young Lloyd or Keaton clowning
(Though you know your Keats and Browning),
You'll say slapstick hath a charm
That's multifarious.
When a fav'rite movie idol
Does a stunt that's suicidal,
Bookworms all declare it's not aesthetic.
Yet when he's hit by a wagon
Or he gets an awful jag on,
Who cares if the scene is not poetic?

I'm tickled silly
And I've got to roar
When they all start to fall
Through the floor;
When, willy-nilly,
A club or a mop
Finds a home on the dome
Of a cop.
My heart's aglow
When they find things are slow
And they start slinging pastry and dough.
Scenes on the beach
Make me holler with glee;
When there's a peach
Losing her dignity;
Whenever they grill 'em,
Whenever they kill 'em,
Oh, that is the "fillem" for me!

Mischa, Jascha, Toscha, Sascha

VERSE I

We really think you ought to know
That we were born right in the middle
Of Darkest Russia.
When we were three years old or so,
We all began to play the fiddle
In Darkest Russia.
When we began,

Our notes were sour—
Until a man
(Professor Auer)
Set out to show us, one and all,
How we could pack them in,
In Carnegie Hall.

REFRAIN I
Temp'ramental Oriental Gentlemen are we:
Mischa, Jascha, Toscha, Sascha—
Fiddle-lee, diddle-lee, dee.
Shakespeare says, "What's in a name?"
With him we disagree.
Names like Sammy, Max or Moe
Never bring the heavy dough
Like Mischa, Jascha, Toscha, Sascha—
Fiddle-lee, diddle-lee, dee.

VERSE 2
Though born in Russia, sure enough,
We're glad that we became relations
Of Uncle Sammy.
For though we play the high-brow stuff,
We also like the syncopations
Of Uncle Sammy.
Our magic bow
Plays Liszt and Schumann;
But then you know
We're only human
And like to shake a leg to jazz.
(Don't think we've not the feelings
Everyone has.)

Temp'ramental Oriental Gentlemen are we:
Mischa, Jascha, Toscha, Sascha—
Fiddle-lee, diddle-lee, dee.
High-brow He-brow may play low-brow
In his privacy.
But when concert halls are packed,
Watch us stiffen up and act
Like Mischa, Jascha, Toscha, Sascha—
Fiddle-lee, diddle-lee, dee.

VERSE 3

You find our pictures ev'rywhere.
They show you we're artistic persons
Who play the fiddle.
When critics hear us, they declare
The rest are all so many worse 'uns
Who play the fiddle.
We're from the best;
The critics said it—
But to the rest
We still give credit.
And so we want it understood
We think that Paganini also was good.

REFRAIN 3

Temp'ramental Oriental Gentlemen are we:
Mischa, Jascha, Toscha, Sascha—
Fiddle-lee, diddle-lee, dee.
We give credit when it's due—
But then you must agree

That outside of dear old Fritz,
All the fiddle-concert hits
Are Mischa, Jascha, Toscha, Sascha—
Fiddle-lee, diddle-lee, dee.

Fascinating Rhythm

VERSE

Got a little rhythm, a rhythm, a rhythm
That pit-a-pats through my brain;
So darn persistent,
The day isn't distant
When it'll drive me insane.
Comes in the morning
Without any warning,
And hangs around me all day.
I'll have to sneak up to it
Someday, and speak up to it.
I hope it listens when I say:

REFRAIN

Fascinating Rhythm,
You've got me on the go!
Fascinating Rhythm,
I'm all a-quiver.

What a mess you're making!
The neighbors want to know
Why I'm always shaking
Just like a flivver.

Each morning I get up with the sun—
Start a-hopping,
Never stopping—
To find at night no work has been done.

I know that
Once it didn't matter—
But now you're doing wrong;
When you start to patter
I'm so unhappy.

Won't you take a day off?
Decide to run along
Somewhere far away off—
And make it snappy!

Oh, how I long to be the man I used to be!
Fascinating Rhythm,
Oh, won't you stop picking on me?

1940s Revision

VERSE
It's like our nation,
A conglomeration;
It isn't any one thing.
Somehow you can't confine it,
And no one could define it.
It's just a rhythm that you sing:

Fascinating Rhythm,
Oh! Never let it stop!
That Manhattan rhythm—
The joint is jumping.

What an orchestration
Of classic and of bop!
Fills you with elation;
Your cares you're dumping!

The taxi horns and planes up above
(Riff and bop it—
Never stop it!)
Join in that symphony that I love.

The nightclubs
Turn you topsy-turvy.
The girls are pure delight.
Ev'ry one so curvy,
You can't resist 'em.

Broadway and its chatter
To music day and night
And to subway clatter,
Oh! How I've missed 'em.

It sends your spirits flying high, won't let you down!
Fascinating Rhythm,
The rhythm of Old New York Town.

Oh, Lady, Be Good!

Listen to my tale of woe,
It's terribly sad, but true:
All dressed up, no place to go,
Each ev'ning I'm awf'ly blue.
I must win some winsome miss;
Can't go on like this.
I could blossom out, I know,
With somebody just like you.
So—

REFRAIN 1

Oh, sweet and lovely lady, be good.
Oh, lady, be good to me!
I am so awf'ly misunderstood,
So, lady, be good to me.
Oh, please have some pity—
I'm all alone in this big city.
I tell you
I'm just a lonesome babe in the wood,
So, lady, be good to me.

VERSE 2

Auburn and brunette and blonde:
I love 'em all, tall or small.
But somehow they don't grow fond;
They stagger but never fall.
Winter's gone, and now it's spring!
Love! where is thy sting?

If somebody won't respond,
I'm going to end it all.
So—

REFRAIN 2
Oh, sweet and lovely lady, be good.
Oh lady, be good to me!
I am so awf'ly misunderstood,
So, lady, be good to me.
This is tulip weather—
So let's put two and two together.
I tell you
I'm just a lonesome babe in the wood,
So, lady, be good to me.

The Half of It, Dearie, Blues

VERSE I

DICK: Each time you trill a song with Bill
Or look at Will, I get a chill—
I'm gloomy.
I won't recall the names of all
The men who fall—It's all appall-
Ing to me.
Of course, I really cannot blame them a bit,
For you're a hit wherever you flit.
I know it's so, but, dearie, oh!
You'll never know the blues that go
Right through me.

> I've got the You-Don't-Know-the-Half-of-It-
> Dearie Blues.
> The trouble is you have so many from whom
> to choose.
> If you should marry
> Tom, Dick, or Harry,
> Life would be the bunk—
> I'd become a monk.
> I've got the You-Don't-Know-the-Half-of-It-
> Dearie Blues!

VERSE 2

SHIRLEY: To Bill and Ben I'd pay atten-
Tion now and then, but really, men
Would bore me.
When I'd begun to think I'd run
And be a nun, I met the one
Man for me.
And now just when the sun is starting to
beam—
You get engaged—Zip! goes a dream!
What will I do away from you?
I feel the future will be blue
And stormy.

REFRAIN 2

> I've got the You-Don't-Know-the-Half-of-It-
> Dearie Blues.
> It may be my heart isn't broken, but there's a
> bruise.

Through you I've known some
Days that were lonesome—
Though you say that I'm
Flirting all the time.
I've got the You-Don't-Know-the-Half-of-It-
    Dearie Blues!

REFRAIN 3

I've got the You-Don't-Know-the-Half-of-It-
    Dearie Blues.
Although I know that love's a gamble, I hate
    to lose.
Life will be duller—
Will have no color;
Jill without a Jack
Makes the future black.
I've got the You-Don't-Know-the-Half-of-It-
    Dearie Blues!

REFRAIN 4

JACK: I've got the You-Don't-Know-the-Half-of-It-
    Dearie Blues.
Will I walk up the aisle or only watch from
    the pews?
With your permission,
My one ambition
Was to go through life
Saying, "Meet the wife."
I've got the You-Don't-Know-the-Half-of-It-
    Dearie Blues!

Little Jazz Bird

Into a cabaret, one fatal day,
A little songbird flew;
Found it so very gay, he thought he'd stay,
Just to get a bird's-eye view.
When he heard the jazz band playing,
He was happy as a lark.
To each measure he kept swaying,
And he stayed till after dark.
Then back to the land he knew, thrilled through and
    through,
He sailed on in the air.
Called all the other birds, and in these words
Started singing then and there.

I'm a little jazz bird,
And I'm telling you to be one, too.
For a little jazz bird
Is in Heaven when it's singing "blue."
I say it with regret,
But you're out of date;
You ain't heard nothin' yet,
Till you syncopate.
When the going is rough,
You will find your troubles all have flown,
If you warble your stuff
Like the moaning of a saxophone.
Just try my recipe,

And I'm sure you'll agree
That a little jazz bird
Is the only kind of bird to be.

The Man I Love

When the mellow moon begins to beam,
Ev'ry night I dream a little dream;
And of course Prince Charming is the theme:
The he
For me.
Although I realize as well as you
It is seldom that a dream comes true,
To me it's clear
That he'll appear.

REFRAIN I
Some day he'll come along,
The man I love;
And he'll be big and strong,
The man I love;
And when he comes my way,
I'll do my best to make him stay.

He'll look at me and smile—
I'll understand;
And in a little while
He'll take my hand;
And though it seems absurd,
I know we both won't say a word.

Maybe I shall meet him Sunday,
Maybe Monday—maybe not;
Still I'm sure to meet him one day—
Maybe Tuesday
Will be my good news day.

He'll build a little home
Just meant for two;
From which I'll never roam—
Who would? Would you?
And so, all else above,
I'm waiting for the man I love.

REFRAIN 2

Some day she'll come along,
The girl I love;
Her smile will be a song,
The girl I love;
And when she comes my way,
I'll do my best to make her stay.

I'll look at her and smile—
She'll understand;
And in a little while
I'll take her hand;
And though it seems absurd,
I know we both won't say a word.

Maybe I will meet her Sunday,
Maybe Monday—maybe not;
Still I'm sure to meet her one day—

Maybe Tuesday
Will be my good news day.

For her I'll do and dare
As ne'er before;
Our hopes and fears we'll share—
For evermore;
And so, all else above,
I'm waiting for the girl I love.

These Charming People

VERSE I

HEN: We must make it our ambition
To live up to our position
As we take our places in society.

AL: When those million-dollar blokes pass,
I will never make a faux pas;
I will show them I am full of pedigree.

TIP-TOES: And the lady isn't born yet
Who can beat me at a lorgnette,
When I'm honoring the op'ra at the Met.

ALL: So if you're not social winners,
Don't invite us to your dinners—
We must warn you we'll be awful hard to get.

REFRAIN I

We'll be like These Charming People,
Putting on the ritz,
Acting as befits

These charming people:
Very debonair,
Full of savoir-faire.
I hear that Mrs. Whoozis
Created quite a stir:
She built a little love nest
For her and her chauffeur.
If these people can be charming,
Then we can be charming, too!

HEN: Please recall, if you've forgotten,
That my father was in cotton,
And my family is truly F.F.V.

AL: Merely social climbing varmints!
Ours was made in undergarments,
So you see before you one who's B.V.D.

TIP-TOES: If that's pedigree, enjoy it!
My old man came from Detroit,
So I'll have you know that I am F.O.B.

ALL: In our veins there runs the true blood!
When we mingle with the blue blood,
The Four Hundred will become Four
Hundred Three.

We'll be like These Charming People,
Putting on the ritz,
Acting as befits
These charming people:
Very debonair,

Full of savoir-faire.
It seems that Mr. Smythe-Smythe
Had no children, till
Some twenty-seven turned up
To listen to the will.
If these people can be charming,
Then we can be charming, too!

Sweet and Low-Down

VERSE

There's a cabaret in *this* city
I can recommend to you;
Peps you up like electricity
When the band is blowing blue.
They play nothing classic, oh no! down there;
They crave nothing else but the low-down there.
If you need a tonic,
And the need is chronic—
If you're in a crisis,
My advice is:

REFRAIN

Grab a cab and go down
To where the band is playing;
Where milk and honey flow down;
Where ev'ry one is saying,
"Blow that Sweet and Low-Down!"

Busy as a beaver,
You'll dance until you totter;
You're sure to get the fever
For nothing could be hotter—
Oh, that Sweet and Low-Down!

Philosopher or deacon,
You simply have to weaken.
Hear those shuffling feet—
You can't keep your seat—
Professor, start your beat!

Come along, get in it—
You'll love the syncopation!
The minute they begin it,
You're shouting to the nation:
"Blow that Sweet and Low-Down!"

Gather Ye Rosebuds

VERSE
Puritans there are who say:
"It is sinful to be gay."
But I cannot share that view—
Life's too short to be blue.
There's no one can stand the gaff
'Less they learn the way to laugh.
I'm for the poet who said one day,
"Gather ye rosebuds while ye may."

The thing to do from ev'ry Monday to Sunday
Is to make of ev'ry one day a fun day.
What's the use of taking time out for sorrow?
You're here today and gone tomorrow.
Why turn down the sun and watchfully wait for
The well-known rainy day?
Rather—Gather rosebuds while ye may.

PATTER

Now Lincoln liked to have his little joke.
And Grant was never seen without a smoke.
When Bobbie Burns and Edgar Allan Poe
Were asked to have a drink, did they say "No"?
You'll find that famous men from A to Z
Were somehow always ready for a spree.
These names have never faded
And anything that they did,
I'm here to tell the world,
Is good enough for me.

REFRAIN 2

This world, I find, is very pleasant to live in
When you learn the thing to do is give in.
Have pajamas made of silk—not of cotton—
For when you're gone, you're soon forgotten.
Why turn down the blue to watchfully wait for
Those well-known skies of gray?
Rather—Gather rosebuds while ye may.

Sunny Disposish

VERSE I

Anytime the thunder starts to rumble down,
Don't let hope tumble down
Or castles crumble down.
If the blues appear, just make the best of them;
Just make a jest of them;
Don't be possessed of them.
At the risk of sounding rather platitudinous—
Here's what I believe should be the attitude in us:

REFRAIN

A sunny disposish
Will always see you through—
When up above the skies are blah
'Stead of being blue.
Mister Trouble makes our faces grow long,
But a smile will have him saying, "So long!"
It really doesn't pay
To be a gloomy pill—
It's absolutely most ridic',
Positively sil'.
The rain may pitter-patter—
It really doesn't matter—
For life can be delish
With a sunny disposish.

VERSE 2

Must confess I like your way of viewing it—
No use in ruing it

When gloom is blueing it.
Taking your advice, the sad and weary'll
Have no material
To be funereal.
It's a thought that they should be swallowing, my dear,
Look at me, already you've a following, my dear.

REPEAT REFRAIN

Do, Do, Do

VERSE I

JIMMY: I remember the bliss
Of that wonderful kiss.
I know that a boy
Could never have more joy
From any little miss.

KAY: I remember it quite;
'Twas a wonderful night.

JIMMY: Oh, how I'd adore it
If you would encore it. Oh—

REFRAIN I

Do, do, do
What you've done, done, done
Before, Baby.
Do, do, do
What I do, do, do
Adore, Baby.

Let's try again,
Sigh again,
Fly again to heaven.
Baby, see
It's A B C—
I love you and you love me.

I know, know, know
What a beau, beau, beau
Should do, Baby;
So, don't, don't, don't
Say it won't, won't, won't
Come true, Baby.

My heart begins to hum—
Dum de dum de dum-dum-dum,
So do, do, do,
What you've done, done, done
Before.

VERSE 2

KAY: Sweets we've tasted before
Cannot stand an encore.
You know that a miss
Who always gives a kiss
Would soon become a bore.

JIMMY: I can't see that at all;
True love never should pall.

KAY: I was only teasing;
What you did was pleasing. Oh—

Do, do, do
What you've done, done, done
Before, Baby.
Do, do, do
What I do, do, do
Adore, Baby.

Let's try again,
Sigh again,
Fly again to heaven.
Baby, see
It's A B C—
I love you and you love me.

JIMMY: You dear, dear, dear
Little dear, dear, dear,
Come here, snappy!
And see, see, see
Little me, me, me
Make you happy.

KAY: My heart begins to sigh—
Di de di de di-di-di,
So do, do, do
What you've done, done, done
Before.

Someone to Watch Over Me

VERSE

There's a saying old
Says that love is blind.
Still, we're often told
"Seek and ye shall find."
So I'm going to seek a certain lad I've had in mind.
Looking ev'rywhere,
Haven't found him yet;
He's the big affair
I cannot forget—
Only man I ever think of with regret.
I'd like to add his initial to my monogram.
Tell me, where is the shepherd for this lost lamb?

REFRAIN

There's a somebody I'm longing to see:
I hope that he
Turns out to be
Someone who'll watch over me.

I'm a little lamb who's lost in the wood;
I know I could
Always be good
To one who'll watch over me.

Although he may not be the man some
Girls think of as handsome,
To my heart he'll carry the key.

Won't you tell him, please, to put on some speed,
Follow my lead?
Oh, how I need
Someone to watch over me.

Male Version

REFRAIN
There's a somebody I've wanted to see:
I hope that she
Turns out to be
Someone who'll watch over me.

I'm a little lamb who's lost in the wood;
I know I could
Always be good
To one who'll watch over me.

She may be far;
She may be nearby;
I'm promising hereby,
To my heart she'll carry the key.

And this world would be like heaven if she'd
Follow my lead.
Oh, how I need
Someone to watch over me.

Strike Up the Band

VERSE

We fought in 1917,
Rum-ta-ta tum-tum-tum!
And drove the tyrant from the scene,
Rum-ta-ta tum-tum-tum!

We're in a bigger, better war
For your patriotic pastime.
We don't know what we're fighting for—
But we didn't know the last time!

So load the cannon! Draw the blade!
Rum-ta-ta tum-tum-tum!
Come on, and join the Big Parade!
Rum-ta-ta tum-tum,
Rum-ta-ta tum-tum,
Rum-ta-ta tum-tum-tum!

REFRAIN I

Let the drums roll out!
(Boom-boom-boom!)
Let the trumpet call!
(Ta-ta-ra-ta-ta-ta-ta!)
While the people shout—
(Hooray!)
Strike up the band!

Hear the cymbals ring!
(Tszing-tszing-tszing!)
Calling one and all
(Ta-ta-ra-ta-ta-ta-ta!)

To the martial swing,
(Left, right!)
Strike up the band!

There is work to be done, to be done—
There's a war to be won, to be won—
Come, you son of a son of a gun—
Take your stand!

Fall in line, yea bo—
Come along, let's go!
Hey, leader, strike up the band!

REFRAIN 2
[*First 14 lines are same as in refrain 1*]
Yankee doo doodle-oo doodle-oo,
We'll come through, doodle-oo doodle-oo,
For the red, white and blue doodle-oo,
Lend a hand.

With our flag unfurled,
We can lick the world!
Hey, leader, strike up the band!

'S Wonderful

VERSE 1
PETER: Life has just begun:
        Jack has found his Jill.
        Don't know what you've done,
        But I'm all a-thrill.

How can words express
Your divine appeal?
You could never guess
All the love I feel.
From now on, lady, I insist,
For me no other girls exist.

'S wonderful! 'S marvelous—
You should care for me!
'S awful nice! 'S Paradise—
'S what I love to see!
You've made my life so glamorous,
You can't blame me for feeling amorous.
Oh, 's wonderful! 'S marvelous—
That you should care for me!

VERSE 2

FRANKIE: Don't mind telling you
In my humble fash
That you thrill me through
With a tender pash.
When you said you care,
'Magine my emosh;
I swore, then and there,
Permanent devosh.
You made all other boys seem blah;
Just you alone filled me with AAH!

'S wonderful! 'S marvelous—
You should care for me!
'S awful nice! 'S Paradise—
'S what I love to see!
My dear, it's four-leaf-clover time;
From now on my heart's working overtime.
Oh, 's wonderful! 'S marvelous—
That you should care for me!

Version sung in "Finale Ultimo"

FRANKIE:	'S wonderful!
PETER:	'S marvelous!
BOTH:	City hall's in view.
FRANKIE:	'S marriage license.
PETER:	'S Niag'ra Falls.
BOTH:	'S 'appiness for two!
DUGSIE:	You've made my life so ting-a-lish;
	I'll even overlook your Eng-a-lish.
JIMMY:	Oh, wedding bells fill the air
	Now that I know you care.

My One and Only

VERSE I

JIMMY: To show affection
In your direction,
You know I'm fit and able.
I more than merely
Love you sincerely;
My cards are on the table.
There must be lots of other men you hypnotize.
All of a sudden, I've begun to realize—
As follows:

REFRAIN

My one and only—
What am I gonna do if you turn me down,
When I'm so crazy over you?
I'd be so lonely—
Where am I gonna go if you turn me down?
Why blacken all my skies of blue?
I tell you I'm not asking any miracle;
It can be done! It can be done!
I know a clergyman who will grow lyrical—
And make us one! And make us one!
So, my one and only—
There isn't a reason why you should turn me
down,
When I'm so crazy over you.

JUNE: It's time you woke up—
It's time you spoke up—
My praise you've never chanted.
Though we're not strangers,
You see the dangers
Of taking me for granted.
And if you cared, you should have told me long
ago;
Dear, otherwise how in the world was I to know?

JIMMY: Well, listen:

REPEAT REFRAIN

The Babbitt and the Bromide

VERSE I

A Babbitt met a Bromide on the avenue one day.
They held a conversation in their own peculiar way.
They both were solid citizens—They both had been
around.
And as they spoke you clearly saw their feet were on the
ground:

REFRAIN I

Hello! How are you?
Howza folks? What's new?
I'm great! That's good!
Ha! Ha! Knock wood!
Well! Well! What say?
Howya been? Nice day!

How's tricks? What's new?
That's fine! How are you?
Nice weather we are having but it gives me such a pain:
I've taken my umbrella, so of course it doesn't rain.
Heigh ho! That's life!
What's new? Howza wife?
Gotta run! Oh, my!
Ta! Ta! Olive oil! Good-bye!

VERSE 2

Ten years went quickly by for both these sub-sti-an-tial
    men,
Then history records one day they chanced to meet again.
That they had both developed in ten years there was no
    doubt,
And so of course they had an awful lot to talk about:

REFRAIN 2

[*Repeat first 8 lines of refrain 1*]
I'm sure I know your face, but I just can't recall your
    name;
Well, how've you been, old boy? You're looking just
    about the same.
[*Repeat last 4 lines of refrain 1*]

VERSE 3

Before they met again some twenty years they had to wait.
This time it happened up above, inside St. Peter's gate.
A harp each one was carrying and both were wearing
    wings,
And this is what they sang as they kept strumming on
    the strings:

[*Repeat first 8 lines of refrain 1*]
You've grown a little stouter since I saw you last, I think.
Come up and see me sometime and we'll have a little
    drink.
[*Repeat last 4 lines of refrain 1*]

The World Is Mine

VERSE

JIMMY: I'm not as rich as Henry Ford is,
           But that doesn't mean a thing!
           Ev'ry rich man often bored is,
           While I'm happy as a king!
           I've not the fame of Mr. Tunney
           Nor the looks of Barrymore,
           Yet to me the world is sunny
           As it never was before.
           Friends like you are dear to me—
           Make me feel content;
           Yes, sir, it is clear to me,
           I'm a lucky gent!

REFRAIN

           Toddling along,
           Making hay,
           Whistling a song
           Through the day—
           Certainly is fine!
           The world is mine!

How can I complain?
Skies are blue.
Haven't lived in vain—
Friends are true—
Certainly a sign
The world is mine!
It's a grand and glorious feeling to be living;
Ev'ry day's that holiday they call Thanksgiving.
Oh, toddling along,
Here and there,
Whistling a song—
Not a care!
Certainly is fine!
The world is mine!

How Long Has This Been Going On?

VERSE I

PETER: As a tot,
When I trot-
Ted in little velvet panties,
I was kissed
By my sist-
Ers, my cousins, and my aunties.
Sad to tell,
It was hell—
An Inferno worse than Dante's.
So, my dear, I swore,
"Never, nevermore!"
On my list,

I insist-
Ed that kissing must be crossed out.
Now I find
I was blind,
And—Oh, lady—how I've lost out!

REFRAIN I

I could cry
Salty tears;
Where have I
Been all these years?
Little wow,
Tell me now:
How long has this been going on?
There were chills
Up my spine,
And some thrills
I can't define.
Listen, sweet,
I repeat:
How long has this been going on?
Oh, I feel that I could melt;
Into heaven I'm hurled.
I know how Columbus felt
Finding another world.
Kiss me once,
Then once more.
What a dunce
I was before!
What a break—
For heaven's sake!
How long has this been going on?

FRANKIE: 'Neath the stars,
At bazaars,
Often I've had to caress men.
Five or ten
Dollars, then,
I'd collect from all those yes-men.
Don't be sad;
I must add
That they meant no more than chessmen.
Darling, can't you see—
'Twas for charity?
Though these lips
Have made slips,
I was never really serious.
Who'd 'a' thought
I'd be brought
To a state that's so delirious?

REFRAIN 2

I could cry
Salty tears;
Where have I
Been all these years?
Listen, you—
Tell me, do:
How long has this been going on?
What a kick—
How I buzz!
Boy, you click
As no one does!

Hear me, sweet,
I repeat:
How long has this been going on?
Dear, when in your arms I creep—
That divine rendezvous—
Don't wake me if I'm asleep,
Let me dream that it's true.
Kiss me twice,
Then once more—
That makes thrice;
Let's make it four!
What a break—
For heaven's sake!
How long has this been going on?

New York Serenade

VERSE

Since I came from Romanza,
I've heard many a serenade.
Fellows there sing a stanza
When they're wooing a pretty maid.
But there's one that's better far
Than any old tune on an old guitar;
It's the serenade you hear
When you land on a New York pier.

Ten thousand steamboats hootin'—
A million taxis tootin'—
What a song! What a song!
That dear old New York Serenade!
Just hear those rivets rattling—
And hear that traffic battling—
Come along, come along and hear it played.
Ev'ry corner has bands moaning—
Jazz bands groaning all night long.
Even though your nerves they shatter
With their clatter,
It really doesn't matter, matter, matter, matter, matter!
matter!
So keep your peace and quiet—
Give me that good old riot!
Come along and hear that New York Serenade!

I've Got a Crush on You

VERSE

NAT: How glad the many millions
Of Annabelles and Lillians
Would be
To capture me.
But you had such persistence
You wore down my resistance;
I fell—
And it was swell.

POLLY: You're my big and brave and handsome Romeo.
        How I won you I shall never, never know.

NAT: It's not that you're attractive—
        But oh, my heart grew active
        When you
        Came into view.

REFRAIN I

        I've got a crush on you, Sweetie Pie.
        All the day and nighttime
        Hear me sigh.
        I never had the least notion
        That I could fall with so much emotion.

        Could you coo,
        Could you care
        For a cunning cottage we could share?
        The world will pardon my mush
        'Cause I've got a crush,
        My baby, on you.

REFRAIN 2

POLLY: I've got a crush on you, Sweetie Pie.
        All the day and nighttime
        Hear me sigh.
        This isn't just a flirtation:
        We're proving that there's predestination.

        I could coo,
        I could care
        For that cunning cottage we could share.

Your mush I never shall shush
'Cause I've got a crush,
My baby, on you.

I Don't Think I'll Fall in Love Today

VERSE I

ANN: Just think of what love leads to:
Maybe to marriage—maybe divorce.

NEIL: Into a jam love speeds two;
It may be Nature's course,
But we mustn't be
Like the other sheep.

ANN: Better far if we
Look before we leap.

BOTH: Perhaps it's better after all
If we don't answer Nature's call.

REFRAIN I

NEIL: Who knows if we'd agree?
You like you and I like me.
I don't think I'll fall in love today.

ANN: When evening shadows creep,
I like dancing—

NEIL: I like sleep.
I don't think I'll fall in love today.

ANN: Still it might be fun to bring
Your carpet slippers;
When the dinner bell would ring,
I'd serve a can of kippers.

NEIL: Don't you know how to cook?

ANN: I could look in a book.

NEIL: I don't think I'll fall in love today.

VERSE 2

NEIL: Love is a fever chronic;
We can avoid it—Why take a chance?

ANN: Safer to be platonic;
Why burn up with romance?

NEIL: Adam without Eve
Happiness had known,
So suppose we leave
Well enough alone.

ANN: Imagine signing up for life,
Then finding peas roll off his knife.

REFRAIN 2

NEIL: D'you sleep with window shut?

ANN: Window shut.

NEIL: Charming, but—
I don't think I'll fall in love today.

ANN: Did you pick that cravat?

NEIL: I did that.

ANN: Here's your hat.
I don't think I'll fall in love today.

BOTH: It's as clear as A B C
We're not agreeing;
Incompatability
The judge would be decreeing.
When all is said and done,
Seems we two will never be one.
Let's, oh, let's not fall in love today!

ANN: Do you play bridge or whist?

NEIL: I like pinochle.

ANN: I insist—
I don't think I'll fall in love today.

NEIL: To what symphonies do you go?

ANN: All I know
Is "Vo-do-de-o!"

NEIL: I don't think I'll fall in love today.
Is the combination wrong?
I've wondered lately.

ANN: We should never get along—
Not even companionately.

BOTH: When all is said and done,
Dear, we two will never make one.
Let's, oh, let's not fall in love today!

What Causes That?

VERSE

NAT: You're so full of trickery—
Life is bitter as chicory;
Bitterness fills my cup.

POLLY: I'm sorry you brought that up.

NAT: Once I thought I'd search around
For the Little Church Around
The Corner. But now, I see
It never was meant to be.

POLLY: Once you used to praise me—
Why are you so high hat?
Big boy, you amaze me!
Tell me, what causes that?

REFRAIN 1

NAT: When I'm away from you, I start despairing—
You ought to know by now what causes that!
I'm growing balder from the hair I'm tearing—
You ought to know by now what causes that!
When some other chap takes you aside—
Oh gosh, I'm all at sea!
I go contemplating suicide—
You're much too much for me!
You're not so dumb that you don't know the
    answer:
Loving you is what causes that!

REFRAIN 2

NAT: If I should climb the Brooklyn Bridge and jump
    off—
Oh, I suppose you'd ask, "What causes that?"
If I should get a gun and bump this chump
    off—
Oh, I suppose you'd ask, "What causes that?"
POLLY: Really, you don't have to mope around
And burn up as you do;
There's a cannon and a rope around—
There's lots of poison, too.
NAT: I'm very blue of late and there's a reason:
Loving you is what causes that!

Home Blues

VERSE
An American in Paris—
On a holiday.
An American in Paris—
Just a boy at play.
'Mid the magic of the city,
'Mid the scene so gay,
He hears a voice a-calling over the sea,
The voice of Homeland saying, "Come back to me!"
It haunts him—
His thoughts go flying;
It haunts him—
His lonely heart is sighing:

REFRAIN
Home—
That's where the sunshine learned to shine;
Home—
A place that love has made divine;
So my eyes are turning
To where I left this yearning
Heart of mine.
Blues—
I get the blues when I'm away;
Blues—
I hear them calling night and day.
Going back forever—
Oh, never, never, never more to roam—
Your wand'ring boy is coming home!

Soon

VERSE

JIM: I'm making up for all the years
That I waited;
I'm compensated
At last.
My heart is through with shirking;
Thanks to you it's working
Fast.
The many lonely nights and days
When this duffer
Just had to suffer
Are past.

JOAN: Life will be a dream song;
Love will be the theme song.

REFRAIN I

JIM: Soon—the lonely nights will be ended;
Soon—two hearts as one will be blended.
I've found the happiness I've waited for:
The only girl that I was fated for.
Oh! Soon—a little cottage will find us
Safe, with all our cares far behind us.
The day you're mine this world will be in tune.
Let's make that day come soon.

REFRAIN 2

JOAN: Soon—my dear, you'll never be lonely;
Soon—you'll find I live for you only.
When I'm with you who cares what time it is,
Or what the place or what the climate is?

Oh! Soon—our little ship will come sailing
Home, through every storm, never failing.

BOTH: The day you're mine this world will be in tune.
Let's make that day come soon.

Bidin' My Time

VERSE I

Some fellers love to Tip-Toe Through The Tulips;
Some fellers go on Singin' In The Rain;
Some fellers keep on Paintin' Skies With Sunshine;
Some fellers keep on Swingin' Down The Lane—
But—

REFRAIN I

I'm Bidin' My Time,
'Cause that's the kinda guy I'm.
While other folks grow dizzy
I keep busy—
Bidin' My Time.

Next year, next year,
Somethin's bound to happen;
This year, this year,
I'll just keep on nappin'—

And—Bidin' My Time,
'Cause that's the kinda guy I'm.
There's no regrettin'
When I'm settin'—
Bidin' My Time.

Some fellers love to Tell It To The Daisies;
Some Stroll Beneath The Honeysuckle Vines;
Some fellers when they've Climbed The Highest
    Mountain
Still keep a-Cryin' For The Carolines—
But—

REFRAIN 2
I'm Bidin' My Time,
'Cause that's the kinda guy I'm—
Beginnin' on a Mond'y
Right through Sund'y,
Bidin' My Time.

Give me, give me
A glass that's full of tinkle;
Let me, let me
Dream like Rip Van Winkle.

He Bided His Time,
And like that Winkle guy I'm.
Chasin' way flies,
How the day flies—
Bidin' My Time!

TAG
I'm Bidin' My Time,
'Cause that's the kinda guy I'm—
Stranger, so long,
I'll just go 'long
Bidin' My Time.

Could You Use Me?

DANNY: Have some pity on an Easterner;
Show a little sympathy.
No one possibly could *be* sterner
Than you have been with me.
There's a job that I'm applying for—
Let me tell it to you thus;
It's a partnership I'm dying for—
Mr. and Mrs. Us!
Before you file it on the shelf,
Let me tell you of myself:

Oh, I'm the chappie
To make you happy:
I'll tie your shoes-ies
And chase your blues-ies;
Oh, lady, would you—
Oh, tell me, could you
Use me?

I'd shake the mat out
And put the cat out!
I'd clean the garret
And feed the parrot.
Oh, lady, would you—
Oh, tell me, could you
Use me?

Do you realize what a good man
You're getting in me?

I'm no Elk or Mason or Woodman
Who gets home at three.

The girls who see me
Grow soft and dreamy,
But I'm a gander
Who won't philander.
Oh, could you use me?
'Cause I certainly could use you!

VERSE 2

MOLLY: There's a chap I know in Mexico
Who's as strong as he can be;
Eating nails and drinking Texaco—
He is the type for me.
There is one in California,
More romantic far than you.
When he sings "Ha-Cha-Cha-Chornia,"
I often think he'll do.
But as for you, sir, I'm afraid
You will never make the grade.

REFRAIN 2

For you're no cowboy;
You're soft—and how!—boy!
I feel no muscle
That's fit for tussle.
I must refuse you;
I cannot use you.
DANNY: 'Scuse me!
MOLLY: No nightlife for you,
The birds would bore you,

The cows won't know you,
A horse would throw you—
You silly man, you,
To ask me, "Can you
Use me?"

Though at love you may be a wizard,
I'm wanting to know:
Could you warm me up in a blizzard,
Say, forty below?

Your ties are freakish;
Your knees are weakish;
Go back to flappers
And highball lappers!
Though you can use me,
I most certainly can't use you!

ENCORE REFRAIN

DANNY: I'd love to rough it!
MOLLY: You'd only muff it!
        You'd better track home;
        You're safer back home.
DANNY: Oh, lady, would you—
        Oh, tell me, could you
        Use me?

If we've no butler,
I'll put the cutler-
Y on the table
As well's I'm able;
I'd slave as few could,
If only you could
Use me.

MOLLY: You don't even know how to lasso
A bull or a steer.

DANNY: When I speak to them in my basso,
They'll worry, don't fear!

I'd be no bother;
I'd make a father
Like no one other—
If you're the mother.
Oh, could you use me?
'Cause I certainly could use you!

Embraceable You

VERSE I

DANNY: Dozens of girls would storm up;
I had to lock my door.
Somehow I couldn't warm up
To one before.
What was it that controlled me?
What kept my love life lean?
My intuition told me
You'd come on the scene.
Lady, listen to the rhythm of my heartbeat,
And you'll get just what I mean.

REFRAIN I

Embrace me,
My sweet embraceable you.
Embrace me,
You irreplaceable you.

Just one look at you—my heart grew tipsy in me;
You and you alone bring out the gypsy in me.
I love all
The many charms about you;
Above all,
I want my arms about you.
Don't be a naughty baby,
Come to papa—come to papa—do!
My sweet embraceable you.

VERSE 2

MOLLY: I went about reciting,
"Here's one who'll never fall!"
But I'm afraid the writing
Is on the wall.
My nose I used to turn up
When you'd besiege my heart;
Now I completely burn up
When you're slow to start.
I'm afraid you'll have to take the consequences;
You upset the apple cart.

REFRAIN 2

Embrace me,
My sweet embraceable you.
Embrace me,
You irreplaceable you.
In your arms I find love so delectable, dear,
I'm afraid it isn't quite respectable, dear.
But hang it!
Come on, let's glorify love!

Ding dang it!
You'll shout "Encore!" if I love.
Don't be a naughty papa,
Come to baby—come to baby—do!
My sweet embraceable you.

ENCORE REFRAIN

DANNY: Dear lady,
My silk-and-lace-able you;
Dear lady,
Be my embraceable you.
You're the only one I love, yes, verily so!
But you're much too shy, unnecessarily so!

MOLLY: I'll try not
To be so formal, my dear.

DANNY: Am I not
A man who's normal, my dear?
There's just one way to cheer me;
Come to papa—come to papa—do!
My sweet embraceable you.

UNUSED REFRAIN

MOLLY: You call me
Your sweet embraceable you;
You call me
Your irreplaceable you.
When you talk that way, it's so delectable, dear,
I'm afraid it isn't quite respectable, dear.
When you, sir,
Act so deliriously,
Then who, sir,

Could take you seriously?
There's no one I'm more fond of,
But I don't see any hurry to
Be your embraceable you.

Sam and Delilah

KATE: Delilah was a floozy;
She never gave a damn.
Delilah wasn't choosy
Till she fell
For a swell
Buckaroo whose name was Sam.

Delilah got in action;
Delilah did her kootch.
She gave him satisfaction,
And he fell
'Neath her spell
With the aid of love and hooch.

But one day—so they tell us—
His true wife he did crave.
Delilah, she got jealous
And she tracked him
And hacked him
And dug for Sam a grave.

It's always that way with passion,
So, cowboy, learn to behave,

Or else you're li'ble to cash in
With no tombstone on your grave.

KATE
AND
CHORUS: Delilah, oh, Delilah!
She's no babe in the wood;
Run, cowboy, run a mile-ah!
If you love
That kind of
Woman, she'll do you no good!

KATE: The sheriff got Delilah.
They swung her from a tree.
The records are on file-ah.
It's distressin'—
But the lesson
Is an easy one to see.

It's always that way with passion,
So, cowboy, learn to behave,
Or else you're li'ble to cash in
With no tombstone on your grave.

KATE
AND
CHORUS: Delilah, oh, Delilah!
She's no babe in the wood;
Run, cowboy, run a mile-ah!
If you love
That kind of
Woman, she'll do you no good!

I Got Rhythm

VERSE

Days can be sunny,
With never a sigh;
Don't need what money
Can buy.

Birds in the tree sing
Their dayful of song.
Why shouldn't we sing
Along?

I'm chipper all the day,
Happy with my lot.
How do I get that way?
Look at what I've got:

REFRAIN

I got rhythm,
I got music,
I got my man—
Who could ask for anything more?

I got daisies
In green pastures,
I got my man—
Who could ask for anything more?

Old Man Trouble,
I don't mind him—
You won't find him
'Round my door.

I got starlight,
I got sweet dreams,
I got my man—
Who could ask for anything more—
Who could ask for anything more?

But Not For Me

VERSE

MOLLY: Old Man Sunshine—listen, you!
Never tell me Dreams Come True!
Just try it—
And I'll start a riot.
Beatrice Fairfax—don't you dare
Ever tell me he will care;
I'm certain
It's the Final Curtain.
I never want to hear
From any cheer-
Ful Pollyannas,
Who tell you Fate
Supplies a Mate—
It's all bananas!

REFRAIN I

They're writing songs of love,
But not for me;
A lucky star's above,
But not for me.

With Love to Lead the Way,
I've found more Clouds of Gray
Than any Russian play
Could guarantee.

I was a fool to fall
And Get That Way;
Heigh ho! Alas! and al-
So Lackaday!

Love ain't done right by Nell;
However—what the hell!
I guess he's not for me.

He's knocking on a door,
But not for me;
He'll plan a two by four,
But not for me.

I've heard that Love's a Game;
I'm puzzled, just the same—
Was I the Moth or Flame . . . ?
I'm all at sea.

It started off so swell,
This "Let's Pretend";
It all began so well;
But what an end!

The climax of a plot
Should be the marriage knot,
But there's no knot for me.

Reprise

GIEBER: They're writing songs of love,
          But not for me;
          A lucky star's above,
          But not for me.

          With Love to Lead the Way,
          I've found more Skies of Gray
          Than any Russian play
          Could guarantee.

          I was a fool to fall
          And Get That Way;
          Heigh ho! Alas! And al-
          So Lackaday!

          Although I can't dismiss
          The mem'ry of her kiss—
          I guess she's not for me.

Delishious

VERSE

What can I say
To sing my praise of you?
I must reveal
The things I feel.
What can I say?
Each lovely phase of you
Just seems to baffle my descriptive powers
Four-and-twenty hours of ev'ry day.

What can I say?
What is the thing
I'd love to sing?
I've said you're marvelous;
I've said you're wonderful;
And yet that's not it.
Now let me see;
I think I've got it!

REFRAIN
You're so delishious
And so caprishious;
I grow ambishious
To have you care for me.

In that connecshion,
You're my selecshion
For true affecshion
For all the time to be.

Oh, I've had one, two, three, four, five,
Six, seven, eight, nine, ten girls before;
But now there's one, and you're the one,
The one girl I adore.

'Cause you're delishious,
And so caprishious,
If I'm repetishious,
It's 'cause you're so delishious.

Love Is Sweeping the Country

VERSE

Why are people gay
All the night and day,
Feeling as they never felt before?
What is the thing
That makes them sing?

Rich man, poor man, thief,
Doctor, lawyer, chief,
Feel a feeling that they can't ignore;
It plays a part
In ev'ry heart,
And ev'ry heart is shouting "Encore!"

REFRAIN

Love is sweeping the country;
Waves are hugging the shore;
All the sexes
From Maine to Texas
Have never known such love before.

See them billing and cooing
Like the birdies above!
Each girl and boy alike,
Sharing joy alike,
Feels that passion'll
Soon be national.
Love is sweeping the country—
There never was so much love!

Patter (*Original Version*)
Spring is in the air—
Each mortal loves his neighbor.
Who's that loving pair?
That's Capital and Labor.

Chevrolet and Ford
Have felt this cosmic urging;
They, with one accord,
Have kissed and now are merging.

Florida and Cal-
Ifornia get together
In a festi*val*
Of oranges and weather.

Boston's upper zones
Are changing all their habits,
And I hear the Cohns
Are taking up the Cabots.

Taximen take dimes
And never curse the traffic,
While the New York *Times*
Adores the New York *Graphic*.

Of Thee I Sing

VERSE

From the Island of Manhattan to the Coast of Gold,
From North to South, from East to West,
You are the love I love the best.

You're the dream girl of the sweetest story ever told;
A dream I've sought both night and day
For years through all the U.S.A.
The star I've hitched my wagon to
Is very obviously you.

REFRAIN

Of thee I sing, baby—
Summer, autumn, winter, spring, baby.
You're my silver lining,
You're my sky of blue;
There's a love-light shining
Just because of you.

Of thee I sing, baby—
You have got that certain thing, baby!
Shining star and inspiration,
Worthy of a mighty nation—
Of thee I sing!

Who Cares?

REPORTERS: We don't want to know about the
                   moratorium,
              Or how near we are to beer,
              Or about the League of Nations,
              Or the seventeen vacations
              You have had since you've been here.

Here's the one thing that the people of
    America
Are beside themselves to know:
They would like to know what's doing
On the lady who is suing
You—Diana Devereaux!

Ev'rybody wants to know:
What about Miss Devereaux?
From the highest to the low:
What about Miss Devereaux?

WINTERGREEN: It's a pleasant day—
That's all I can say!

MARY: Here's the one thing we'll announce:
Love's the only thing that counts!

REPORTERS: People want to know:
What of Devereaux?

WINTERGREEN: When the one you love is near,
Nothing else can interfere.

ALL: When the one you love is near,
Nothing else can interfere.

VERSE

WINTERGREEN: Here's some information
I will gladly give the nation:
I am for the true love;
Here's the only girl I do love.

MARY: I love him and he loves me,
And that's how it will always be,
So what care we about Miss Devereaux?

BOTH: Who cares what the public chatters?
Love's the only thing that matters.

REFRAIN

Who cares
If the sky cares to fall in the sea?
Who cares what banks fail in Yonkers,
Long as you've got a kiss that conquers?
Why should I care?
Life is one long jubilee,
So long as I care for you—
And you care for me.

Sheet Music Verse
Let it rain and thunder!
Let a million firms go under!
I am not concerned with
Stocks and bonds that I've been burned with.

I love you and you love me,
And that's how it will always be.
And nothing else can ever mean a thing.

Who cares what the public chatters?
Love's the only thing that matters.

I've Got To Be There

When I keep seeing things and going places,
My life has color;
Without new songs, without new friends and faces,
'Twould be much duller.

Whenever people step up
To say, "Let's step tonight,"
If I've been low, I pep up;
Again the future's bright!
Whenever there's a party I can go to,
It makes the world seem right!

REFRAIN
When music is playing
And couples are swaying—
Say! I've got to be there!
I've got to be there!

When joy's in the making
And ceilings are shaking
And there's never a care—
I've got to be there!

Check my hat
And throw the stub away!
I'm a lamb
Who's gone astray!

When bottles are popping
And dignity's dropping
And the women are fair—
I've got to be there!

Isn't It a Pity?

VERSE 1

MICHAEL: Why did I wander
Here and there and yonder,
Wasting precious time
For no reason or rhyme?
Isn't it a pity?
Isn't it a crime?

My journey's ended;
Ev'rything is splendid.
Meeting you today
Has given me a
Wonderful idea;
Here I stay!

REFRAIN 1

It's a funny thing;
I look at you—
I get a thrill
I never knew;
Isn't it a pity
We never met before?
Here we are at last!
It's like a dream!
The two of us—
A perfect team!
Isn't it a pity
We never met before?

Imagine all the lonely years we've wasted:
You, with the neighbors—

I, at silly labors;
What joys untasted!
You, reading Heine,
I, somewhere in China.

Happiest of men
I'm sure to be
If only you
Will say to me,
"It's an awful pity,
We never, never met before!"

VERSE 2

ILSE: While you were flitting,
I was busy knitting.
MICHAEL: How did you survive
Waiting till I'd arrive?
ILSE: All my Dresden boyfriends
Were only half-alive.

Sleepy was Hermann,
Fritz was like a sermon,
Hans was such a bore!
MICHAEL: How well I planned it!
ILSE: I couldn't stand it
Anymore!

REFRAIN 2

It's a funny thing;
I look at you—
I get a thrill
I never knew;
Isn't it a pity
We never met before?

Here we are at last!
It's like a dream!
The two of us—
A perfect team—
MICHAEL: For you're more than pretty,
And I have charm galore!

ILSE: Imagine all the lonely years we've wasted:
You, up in Norway—
I, around my doorway.
What joys untasted!
If you'd been handy,
'Twould have been just dandy!

Isn't it a shame
We had to wait?
MICHAEL: But thank the Lord
It's not too late!
BOTH: Still, it's such a pity
We never, never met before!

REFRAIN 3
ILSE: Love your funny smile,
Your twinkling eye.
MICHAEL: That's very nice—
For—so do I!
BOTH: Isn't it a pity
We never met before?

MICHAEL: Put your hand in mine—
A perfect fit!
We never knew—
Just think of it!

BOTH: Isn't it a pity
We never met before?

MICHAEL: Imagine all the lonely years I've wasted:
Fishing for salmon,
Losing at backgammon.
ILSE: What joys untasted!
My nights were sour
Spent with Schopenhauer.

BOTH: Let's forget the past!
Let's both agree
That I'm for you
And you're for me—
And it's such a pity
We never, never met before!

Freud and Jung and Adler

VERSE

TWO
DOCTORS: If a person starts to quiver
Through cirrhosis of the liver,
We can't be bothered with that sort of thing
at all.

TWO
OTHERS: But how eagerly do we go
To an egg who has an ego
Or a brain that's scrambled 'way beyond recall.

TWO
OTHERS: We don't cure appendicitis
           Or the mumps or laryngitis—
           That is not the kind of service that we sell.

ALL: But we're always on location
           When it's mental aberration,
           For that pays twice as well.

NURSES: You must know that when a
           Doctor's from Vienna—
           That pays twice as well!

REFRAIN I

DOCTORS: Doctor Freud and Jung and Adler, Adler and
                 Jung and Freud—
           Six psychoanalysts, we!
           Just let us make one diagnosis—
           We'll know *was loss is*"!
           Doctor Freud and Jung and Adler, Adler and
                 Jung and Freud.
           Visiting hours, nine to three.
           If you ever had the dream that Mrs. Grundy's
           Always keeping her eye on you on Sund'ys,
           And you suddenly find you're standing in
                 your undies—
           We are positive that you had better see
           Doctor Freud and Jung and Adler, Adler and
                 Jung and Freud—
           Six sex psychos, we!

[*Repeat refrain 1, lines 1–6*]

> If you've any mental problem that
>> perplexes—
> If there's anything that's wrong with your
>> reflexes—
> If you're really not certain as to which your
>> sex is—
> We are positive that you had better see
> Doctor Freud and Jung and Adler, Adler and
>> Jung and Freud—
> Six sex psychos, we!

Union Square *and*
Down With Everyone Who's Up

"Union Square"

ENSEMBLE: Our hearts are in communion
When we gather down on Union
Square, heigh ho!
When whiskers are unshaven,
One can always find a haven
There, heigh ho!
Though some may prefer the charming
    Bronnix,
Though some sing of dainty Sutton Place,
'Tis here we discover all the tonics
That cure all the problems of the race.
Oh, on boxes they put soap in,

How we love it in the open
Air, heigh ho!
We may not fill our stomics,
But we're full of economics
Down on Union Square!
Down here on Union Square!

[*Agitators, led by Kruger, march on. Their tone is sharper, and grows more strident as the number continues*]

"Down With Everyone Who's Up"

KRUGER: Conditions as they are
Cannot go very far;
The world must move and we are here to
move it!
The Brotherhood of Man
Is crying for a plan;
So here's my plan—I know you can't
improve it!

ALL: Conditions as they are
Cannot go very far;
So, listen to his plan
For Man!

[*softly*]

Down, down, down, down,
Down, down, down, down.

KRUGER: Down with one and one make two!
Down with ev'rything in view!
Down with all majorities;
Likewise all minorities!
Down with you and you and you!

ALL: Down with one and one make three!
Down with all of us, says he.

KRUGER: Somehow I abominate
Anything you nominate!

ALL: Ev'rything from A, B, C to X, Y, Z!

KRUGER: That's the torch we're going to get the
flame from!
If you don't like it, why don't you go back
where you came from?

ALL: If you don't like it, why don't you go back
where you came from!
If you don't like it, why don't you go back
where you came from!

KRUGER: Let's tear down the House of Morgan!
ALL: House of Morgan!
KRUGER: Let's burn up the Roxy organ!
ALL: Roxy organ!

KRUGER: Down with Curry and McCooey!
ALL: And McCooey!
KRUGER: Down with chow mein and chop suey!
ALL: And chop suey!

KRUGER: Down with music by Stravinsky!
ALL: By Stravinsky!
KRUGER: Down with shows except by Minsky!
ALL: Up with Minsky!

KRUGER: Happiness will fill our cup
When it's "Down with ev'rything that's up!"
ALL: When it's "Down with ev'rything that's up!"

KRUGER:	Down with books by Dostoyevsky!
ALL:	Dostoyevsky!
KRUGER:	Down with Boris Thomashefsky!
ALL:	Thomashefsky!
KRUGER:	Down with Balzac! Down with Zola!
ALL:	Down with Zola!
KRUGER:	Down with pianists who play "Nola"!

[*Entire stage dances to "Nola"*]

KRUGER:	Down with all the upper classes!
ALL:	Upper classes!
KRUGER:	Might as well include the masses!
	'Clude the masses!
KRUGER:	Happiness will fill our cup
	When it's "Down with ev'ryone who's up!"
ALL:	When it's "Down with ev'ryone who's up!"
KRUGER:	So down with this! And down with that!
	And down with ev'rything in view!
	The hell with this! The hell with that!
	The hell with you and you and you!
ONE HALF OF THE MOB:	The hell with who?
KRUGER:	The hell with you!
OTHER HALF:	The hell with whom?
KRUGER:	The hell with youm!
ALL:	The hell with you and you and you!

[*All square off. A free-for-all follows. They are struggling on the floor when a policeman enters, blows whistle. They get up, flick off the dust. All, including the policeman, saunter off, singing:*]

ENSEMBLE: Our hearts are in communion
              When we gather down on Union
              Square, heigh ho!
              When whiskers are unshaven,
              One can always find a haven
              There, heigh ho!
              Though some may prefer the charming
                  Bronnix,
              Though some sing of dainty Sutton Place,
              'Tis here we discover all the tonics
              That cure all the problems of the race.
              Oh, on boxes they put soap in,
              How we love it in the open
              Air, heigh ho!
              We may not fill our stomics,
              But we're full of economics
              Down on Union Square!
              Down here on Union Square!

Mine

WINTERGREEN: My good friends, don't praise *me*!
              I owe it all to the little woman—
              This little woman, *my* little woman—
ENSEMBLE: *His* little woman!
WINTERGREEN: She's the reason for my success.
              Why, when I think how we suffered
                  together—
MARY: Worried together, struggled together—

WINTERGREEN:	Stood together together!
	I grow so sentimental, I'm afraid
	I've got to burst into song.
ENSEMBLE:	Please do!
	We'd love to know how you feel about her
	And how she feels about you.
WINTERGREEN:	Mine, love is mine,
	Whether it rain or storm or shine.
	Mine, you are mine,
	Never another valentine.
	And I am yours,
	Tell me that I'm yours,
	Show me that smile my heart adores.
	Mine, more than divine
	To know that love like yours is mine!

[*Ensemble sings as Wintergreen and Mary repeat "Mine" softly*]

ENSEMBLE:	The point they're making in the song
	Is that they more than get along;
	And he is not ashamed to say
	She made him what he is today.
	It does a person good to see
	Such happy domesticity;
	The way they're making love, you'd swear
	They're not a married pair.
	He says, no matter what occurs,
	Whatever he may have is hers;
	The point that *she* is making is
	Whatever *she* may have is his.

ALL: Mine, more than divine
        To know that love like yours is mine!

[*Both melodies are sung together.*]

It Ain't Necessarily So

SPORTIN' LIFE: It ain't necessarily so.
ALL: It ain't necessarily so.
SPORTIN' LIFE: De t'ings dat yo li'ble
        To read in de Bible—
        It ain't necessarily so.

        Li'l' David was small, but—oh my!
ALL: Li'l' David was small, but—oh my!
SPORTIN' LIFE: He fought Big Goliath
        Who lay down and dieth—
        Li'l' David was small, but—oh my!

        Wadoo!
ENSEMBLE: Wadoo!
SPORTIN' LIFE: Zim bam boddle-oo!
ENSEMBLE: Zim bam boddle-oo!
SPORTIN' LIFE: Hoodle ah da wah da!
ENSEMBLE: Hoodle ah da wah da!
SPORTIN' LIFE: Scatty wah!
ENSEMBLE: Scatty wah!
SPORTIN' LIFE: Yeah!

        Oh, Jonah, he lived in de whale.
ALL: Oh, Jonah, he lived in de whale.

SPORTIN' LIFE: Fo' he made his home in
Dat fish's abdomen—
Oh Jonah, he lived in de whale.

Li'l' Moses was found in a stream.
ALL: Li'l' Moses was found in a stream.
SPORTIN' LIFE: He floated on water
Till Ole Pharaoh's daughter
She fished him, she *says*, from dat
stream.

Wadoo!
ENSEMBLE: Wadoo!
SPORTIN' LIFE: Zim bam boddle-oo!
ENSEMBLE: Zim bam boddle-oo!
SPORTIN' LIFE: Hoodle ah da wah da!
ENSEMBLE: Hoodle ah da wah da!
SPORTIN' LIFE: Scatty wah!
ENSEMBLE: Scatty wah!
SPORTIN' LIFE: Yeah!

SPORTIN' LIFE: It ain't necessarily so,
ALL: It ain't necessarily so.
SPORTIN' LIFE: Dey tell all you chillun
De Debble's a villun
But 'tain't necessarily so.

To get into Hebben
Don't snap fo' a sebben—
Live clean! Don' have no fault!
Oh, I takes dat gospel
Whenever it's pos'ple—
But wid a grain of salt!

	Methus'lah lived nine hundred years.
ALL:	Methus'lah lived nine hundred years.
SPORTIN' LIFE:	But who calls dat livin'
	When no gal'll give in
	To no man what's nine hundred years?

	I'm preachin' dis sermon to show
	It ain't nessa, ain't nessa,
	Ain't nessa, ain't nessa—
ALL:	Ain't necessarily so!

Encore Limerick

'Way back in five thousand B.C.
Ole Adam an' Eve had to flee.
Sure, dey did dat deed in
De Garden of Eden—
But why chasterize you an' me?

Island in the West Indies

VERSE

Let's both of us pack up,
Sail far from it all;
Tired having to back up
To the wall.
I know of a place where
Life really is fun—
Where days are golden
And you're beholden

To none.
Let's take passage and run!

Oh, there's an island down in the West Indies
Ten dollars can buy;
Away from Reuben's and from Lindy's—
'Neath a tropic,
Kaleidoscopical sky.

We'll lie around all day and just be lazy—
The world far behind;
(If that's not heaven then I'm crazy)
With no taxes
And with no axes to grind.

No traffic jams
Under the palm trees by the sea;
With breadfruit and yams
We'll never need the A & P.

In that romantic isle in the West Indies—
No airplanes above—
We'll watch the turtles at their shindies,
You an' me an'
The Caribbean
And love.

Second Ending
We'll watch the turtles at their shindies;
Learn the lingos
Of pink flamingos;

Where nothing's immoral
'Way out on the coral;
All day we'll ramble
Where starfish gambol;
Just you an' me an'
The Caribbean
And love.

Words Without Music

VERSE

It's an old, old, old variation
On the very oldest of themes:
It's the one that starts as flirtation
And that ends in broken dreams;
It's the feeling when he enfolds you,
He'll forget you soon as he's gone—
But, what can you do?
You're in love and you
Hold on.

REFRAIN

Words without music,
Smoke without flame—
Charming phrases
That sing your praises
And call your name.

Night without magic,
Days without end—

Same old story,
The empty glory
Of Let's Pretend.

Had I had an inkling
That he could not be true,
These blues of mine could never start;
But stars above were twinkling,
And then before I knew—
He was locked up in my heart.

I'll hear words without music
All my life long—
Hoping, praying
That what he's saying
Will turn to song.

The Economic Situation

VERSE

I'm tired of keeping up with the economic trends
And the universal problems that perplex;
Oh, tell me where can I find a man who condescends
To show an int'rest in sex.
Affairs of Heart mean nothing to men, of late;
It seems they only go for Affairs of State.

REFRAIN I

It used to be that a girl could get away
With "Aren't you wonderful!"—
But the economic situation has changed all that.

It used to be all you'd ever have to say
Was "Aren't you wonderful!"—
And a man would show his adoration—and you sat pat.

But today if you want to panic a
Guy without using a gun,
You've got to be a *Britannica*
And an almanac rolled into one.

It used to be a girl could get away
With "Aren't you wonderful!"—
But the economic situation has changed all that.

RECITED INTERLUDE
You're sitting with a man on a moonlit veranda—
You've got stars and music and other propaganda—
And what happens? Does he make love? No! We have a
    discussion
About the Effects of the Dynamo on the Russian.

You're looking your best, but he hasn't noticed,
For you're up to your neck in the Taxpayers' Protest.
Your perfume's thirty dollars an ounce and your makeup
    is fresh—
But not for *him* the lure of the flesh.

Discussing Germanism,
And Economic Determinism,
And H. G. Wells' latest Utopia,
And Mr. Borah on Ethiopia,
And Morgenthau on the Surtax,
And Jaeckel on the Fur Tax,
And what about Brooklyn—Will Roosevelt carry it?
And the Effect of Eccles and Ickes on the Proletariat.

With glittering eyes we get to the Underplowing of
     Cotton,
And Man Forgotten . . .
Forgotten Man, hell!
What about the Forgotten Gel?
But no! He throws you the Supreme Court's Latest
     Decisions,
And you retaliate with Franco-Polish Treaty Revisions,
And he Five-Five-Threes you about Japan,
And you knock him down with the Townsend Plan,
And he gives you Wallace and Tugwell until it hurts,
And by the time he leaves you're screaming, "Nerts!
     Nerts! Nerts!"

REFRAIN 2
It used to be that a girl could get away
With "Aren't you wonderful!"—
But the economic situation has changed all that.

It used to be all you'd ever have to say
Was "Aren't you wonderful!"—
There was never need in conversation of tit for tat.

But today we are mediocrities
If we can't get an A plus
On questions that Plato and Socrates
And Disraeli wouldn't dare discuss.

Oh, turn again to the day when baby chatter was
     effectual,
And you didn't have to be a goddamned highbrowed
     intellectual
With the men!

I Can't Get Started

Ziegfeld Follies *of 1936 Version*

HOPE: [*spoken*]
Wasn't it a wonderful dinner?

ARDEN: Oh, all right. I've had better. Well, good night.
[*Starts to leave*]

HOPE: Wasn't it funny how the customers recognized me? You know, I had to sign forty autographs.

ARDEN: So what? Well, good night. Here, taxi!

HOPE: Gosh, I can't seem to get to first base with you. Never a smile, never a kind word. Good God, what would I have to give you for a kiss?

ARDEN: Ronald Colman.

HOPE: You know, we were in the same class at Oxford.

ARDEN: Well, you're not in his class now.

HOPE: Listen, on six continents and seven oceans, I'm tops. Everybody is crazy about me. And I'm crazy about you. I love you so. I want you so.

ARDEN: So what? Well—

BOTH: Good night.

VERSE

HOPE: I'm a glum one; it's explainable:
I met someone unattainable;
Life's a bore,

The world is my oyster no more.
All the papers, where I led the news
With my capers, now will spread the news:
"Superman
Turns Out to Be Flash in the Pan."

REFRAIN 1

I've flown around the world in a plane;
I won the race from Newport to Maine;
The North Pole I have charted,
But can't get started with you.

Around a golf course I'm under par,
The Theatre Guilders want me to star;
I've got a house—a showplace—
But I get no place with you.

You're so supreme,
Lyrics I write of you;
Scheme
Just for a sight of you;
Dream
Both day and night of you,
And what good does it do?

I've been consulted by Franklin D.
And Greta Garbo's asked me to tea,
And yet I'm brokenhearted
'Cause I can't get started with you.

REFRAIN 2

I do a hundred yards in ten flat;
The Duke of Kent has copied my hat;

With queens I've à la carted,
But can't get started with you.

When Democrats are all in a mess,
I hear Jim Farley's call of distress,
And I help him maneuver,
But I'm just Hoover to you.

When first we met—
How you elated me!
Pet!
You devastated me!
Yet,
Now you've deflated me
Till you're my Waterloo.

When J. P. Morgan bows, I just nod;
Green Pastures wanted me to play God.
The Siamese Twins I've parted,
But I can't get started with you.

REFRAIN 3

The Himalaya Mountains I climb;
I'm written up in *Fortune* and *Time*.
New Yorker did my profile ["*pro-feel*"]
But I've had no feel from you.

There's always "Best regards and much love"
From Mr. Lehman—you know, the Gov;
I go to ev'ry state ball,
But I'm just behind the eight ball with you.

Oh, tell me why
Am I no kick to you?
I,

Who'd always stick to you?
Fly
Through thin and thick to you?
Tell me why I'm taboo!

Oh, what a man you're keeping at bay;
I use a pound of Lifebuoy each day;
But you've got me downhearted
'Cause I can't, I can't, I can't, I can't,
I can't get started with you.

ARDEN: [*spoken*]
            Oh well, what can I lose?
[*She turns resignedly and permits him to embrace her. A long
kiss follows. Her lack of interest becomes ardent cooperation.
Never has she met his equal. She holds him at arm's length*]
            My God! You're wonderful! You're marvelous!
  HOPE: That's all I wanted to know! Well, good night!
[*Jauntily he walks off, leaving her flabbergasted*]
[*Blackout*]

Tryout Version sung by Judy Canova
REFRAIN 4
            I've sold my kisses at a bazaar,
            And after me they've named a cigar.
            But lately, how I've smarted—
            I can't get started with you.

            Why, Lucius Beebe quotes me on styles,
            And Pepsodent used one of my smiles.
            The Vanderbilts I visit,
            But say, what *is* it with you?

Oh, tell me why
Am I no kick to you?
I,
Who'd always stick to you?
Fly
Through thin and thick to you?
Tell me why I'm taboo!

In 1929, I sold short;
In England, I'm presented at court,
But you've got me downhearted,
'Cause I can't, I can't, I can't, I can't, I can't,
I can't get started with you.

Published Version

VERSE
[*as in* Follies *version*]

REFRAIN I
I've flown around the world in a plane;
I've settled revolutions in Spain;
The North Pole I have charted,
But can't get started with you.

Around a golf course I'm under par,
And all the movies want me to star;
I've got a house, a showplace—
But I get no place with you.

You're so supreme,
Lyrics I write of you;
Scheme

Just for a sight of you;
Dream
Both day and night of you,
And what good does it do?

In 1929, I sold short;
In England, I'm presented at court,
But you've got me downhearted
'Cause I can't get started with you.

REFRAIN 2
I do a hundred yards in ten flat;
The Prince of Wales has copied my hat;
With queens I've à la carted,
But can't get started with you.

The leading tailors follow my styles.
And toothpaste ads all feature my smiles.
The Astorbilts I visit,
But say, what *is* it with you?

When first we met—
How you elated me!
Pet!
You devastated me!
Yet,
Now you've deflated me
Till you're my Waterloo.

I've sold my kisses at a bazaar,
And after me they've named a cigar.
But lately, how I've smarted—
'Cause I can't get started with you.

Female Version

I'm a glum one; it's explainable:
I met someone unattainable.
Life's a bore,
The world is my oyster no more.
All the papers, where I led the news
With my capers, now will spread the news:
"Super Gal
Is Punchy and Losing Morale!"

REFRAIN I

I've flown around the world in a plane;
I'm known from California to Maine;
With kings I've à la carted—
But can't get started with you.

Around a golf course I'm under par,
And all the movies want me to star;
I've got a house—a showplace—
But I get no place with you.

You're so supreme,
Lyrics I write of you;
Scheme
Just for a sight of you;
Dream
Both day and night of you.
And what good does it do?

The market trembles when I sell short;
In England, I'm presented at court.
But you've got me downhearted
'Cause I can't get started with you.

When I sell kisses at a bazaar,
The wolves line up from nearby and far;
Their methods I have charted,
But I can't get started with you.

The millionaires that I have turned down
Would stretch from London to New York Town;
The upper crust I visit,
But say, what *is* it—with you?

When first we met—
How you elated me!
Pet!

You devastated me!
Yet—
Now you've deflated me
Till you're my Waterloo.

Though beauty columns ask my advice,
Though I was "Miss America" twice,
Still, you've got me outsmarted
'Cause I can't get started with you.

The Himalaya Mountains I climb;
I'm written up in *Fortune* and *Time*.
I dig the Fourth Dimension,
But no attention from you!

There's always "Best regards and much love"
From Mr. Dewey—you know, the Gov;
I'm there at ev'ry state ball
But behind the eight ball with you.

Oh, tell me why
Am I no kick to you?
I,
Who'd always stick to you?
Fly
Through thin and thick to you?
Tell me why I'm taboo!

Good grief! I'm not exactly a clod!
Green Pastures wanted me to play God!
The Siamese Twins I've parted—
But I can't get started with you.

Duet Version

VERSE

BING
CROSBY: I'm a glum one; it's explainable:
    I met someone unattainable;
    Life's a bore,
    The world is my oyster no more.

ROSEMARY I'm a glum one; it's explainable:
CLOONEY: All the papers, where you led the news
    With your capers, now will spread the news:
    "Superman
    Turns Out to Be Flash in the Pan."

REFRAIN I

CROSBY: The Himalaya Mountains I climb;
CLOONEY: You're written up in *Fortune* and *Time*.
CROSBY: I dig the Fourth Dimension—
    But no attention from you.

CROSBY: When I sell kisses at a bazaar,
CLOONEY: The gals line up from near and from far.
CROSBY: Their methods I have charted,
But can't get started with you.

CROSBY: Oh, tell me why
Am I no kick to you?
I,
Who'd always stick to you?
Fly
Through thin and thick to you?
Tell me why I'm taboo.

CLOONEY: The market trembles when you sell short.
CROSBY: In England, I'm presented at court.
CLOONEY: With kings you've à la carted—
CROSBY: Still, I can't get started with you.

REFRAIN 2 (HALF CHORUS)
CLOONEY: When first we met—
How you elated me!
Pet!
You devastated me!
CROSBY: Yet—
How you've deflated me
Till you're my Waterloo.

CROSBY: Good grief! I'm not exactly a clod.
When Elvis Presley bows, I just nod.
CLOONEY: You're asked to every state ball.
CROSBY: Still, I'm behind the eight ball.
CLOONEY: Your dad's a Wall Street banker.
CROSBY: Still, I'm just a tanker.

CLOONEY:	You sum up what a gent is.
CROSBY:	Still, I'm non compos mentis with you.
BOTH:	No, I (you) just can't get started with you (me).

(I've Got) Beginner's Luck

VERSE

At any gambling casino
From Monte Carlo to Reno,
They tell you that a beginner
Comes out a winner.
Beginner fishing for flounder
Will catch a seventeen-pounder.
That's what I always heard
And always thought absurd,
But now I believe ev'ry word.
For—

REFRAIN

I've got beginner's luck:
The first time that I'm in love,
I'm in love with you.
(Gosh, I'm lucky!)
I've got beginner's luck:
There never was such a smile
Or such eyes of blue!
(Gosh, I'm fortunate!)
This thing we've begun

Is much more than a pastime,
For this time is the one
Where the first time is the last time!
I've got beginner's luck,
Lucky through and through,
'Cause the first time that I'm in love,
I'm in love with you.

They All Laughed

VERSE

The odds were a hundred to one against me,
The world thought the heights were too high to climb.
But people from Missouri never incensed me:
Oh, I wasn't a bit concerned,
For from hist'ry I had learned
How many, many times the worm had turned.

REFRAIN I

They all laughed at Christopher Columbus
When he said the world was round;
They all laughed when Edison recorded sound.

They all laughed at Wilbur and his brother
When they said that man could fly;
They told Marconi
Wireless was a phony—
It's the same old cry!

They laughed at me wanting you,
Said I was reaching for the moon;
But oh, you came through—
Now they'll have to change their tune.

They all said we never could be happy,
They laughed at us—and how!
But ho, ho, ho—
Who's got the last laugh now!

REFRAIN 2
They all laughed at Rockefeller Center—
Now they're fighting to get in;
They all laughed at Whitney and his cotton gin.

They all laughed at Fulton and his steamboat,
Hershey and his choc'late bar.
Ford and his Lizzie
Kept the laughers busy—
That's how people are!

They laughed at me wanting you—
Said it would be Hello! Good-bye!
But oh, you came through—
Now they're eating humble pie.

They all said we'd never get together—
Darling, let's take a bow,
For ho, ho, ho—
Who's got the last laugh—
He, he, he—
Let's at the past laugh—
Ha, ha, ha—
Who's got the last laugh now?

They Can't Take That Away From Me

VERSE
Our romance won't end on a sorrowful note,
Though by tomorrow you're gone;
The song is ended, but as the songwriter wrote,
"The melody lingers on."
They may take you from me,
I'll miss your fond caress.
But though they take you from me,
I'll still possess:

REFRAIN
The way you wear your hat,
The way you sip your tea,
The mem'ry of all that—
No, no! They can't take that away from me!

The way your smile just beams,
The way you sing off key,
The way you haunt my dreams—
No, no! They can't take that away from me!

We may never, never meet again
On the bumpy road to love,
Still I'll always, always keep
The mem'ry of—

The way you hold your knife,
The way we danced till three,
The way you've changed my life—
No, no! They can't take that away from me!
No! They can't take that away from me!

Let's Call the Whole Thing Off

VERSE
Things have come to a pretty pass—
Our romance is growing flat,
For you like this and the other,
While I go for this and that.
Goodness knows what the end will be;
Oh, I don't know where I'm at. . . .
It looks as if we two will never be one.
Something must be done.

REFRAIN I
You say eether and I say eyether,
You say neether and I say nyther;
Eether, eyether, neether, nyther—
Let's call the whole thing off!

You like potato and I like po-tah-to;
You like tomato and I like to-mah-to;
Potato, po-tah-to, tomato, to-mah-to—
Let's call the whole thing off!

But oh, if we call the whole thing off, then we must part.
And oh, if we ever part, then that might break my heart.

So, if you like pajamas and I like pa-jah-mas,
I'll wear pajamas and give up pa-jah-mas.
For we know we
Need each other, so we
Better call the calling off off.
Let's call the whole thing off!

You say laughter and I say lawfter,
You say after and I say awfter;
Laughter, lawfter, after, awfter—
Let's call the whole thing off!

You like vanilla and I like vanella,
You, sa's'parilla and I sa's'parella;
Vanilla, vanella, choc'late, strawb'ry—
Let's call the whole thing off!

But oh, if we call the whole thing off, then we must part.
And oh, if we ever part, then that might break my heart.

So, if you go for oysters and I go for ersters,
I'll order oysters and cancel the ersters.
For we know we
Need each other, so we
Better call the calling off off.
Let's call the whole thing off!

I Can't Be Bothered Now

VERSE

Music is the magic that makes everything sunshiny;
Dancing makes my troubles all seem tiny.
When I'm dancing I don't care if this old world stops
     turning,
Or if my bank is burning,
Or even if Roumania
Wants to fight Albania.

I'm not upset;
I refuse to fret.

Bad news, go 'way!
Call 'round some day
In March or May—
I can't be bothered now.

My bonds and shares
May fall downstairs—
Who cares? Who cares?
I'm dancing and I can't be bothered now.

I'm up among the stars;
On earthly things I frown.
I'm throwing off the bars
That held me down.

I'll pay the piper
When times are riper.
Just now, I shan't—
Because you see I'm dancing and I can't—
Be bothered now.

Things Are Looking Up

VERSE

If I should suddenly start to sing
Or stand on my head—or anything,
Don't think that I've lost my senses;

It's just that my happiness finally commences.
The long, long ages of dull despair
Are turning into thin air,
And it seems that suddenly I've
Become the happiest man alive.

REFRAIN
Things are looking up!
I've been looking the landscape over
And it's covered with four-leaf clover.
Oh, things are looking up
Since love looked up at me.

Bitter was my cup—
But no more will I be the mourner,
For I've certainly turned the corner.
Oh, things are looking up
Since love looked up at me.

See the sunbeams—
Ev'ry one beams
Just because of you.
Love's in session,
And my depression
Is unmistakably through.

Things are looking up!
It's a great little world we live in!
Oh, I'm happy as a pup
Since love looked up
At me.

A Foggy Day (in London Town)

VERSE

I was a stranger in the city.
Out of town were the people I knew.
I had that feeling of self-pity:
What to do? What to do? What to do?
The outlook was decidedly blue.
But as I walked through the foggy streets alone,
It turned out to be the luckiest day I've known.

REFRAIN

A foggy day in London Town
Had me low and had me down.
I viewed the morning with alarm.
The British Museum had lost its charm.
How long, I wondered, could this thing last?
But the age of miracles hadn't passed,
For, suddenly, I saw you there—
And through foggy London Town
The sun was shining ev'rywhere.

Nice Work If You Can Get It

VERSE

The man who lives for only making money
Lives a life that isn't necessarily sunny;
Likewise the man who works for fame—
There's no guarantee that time won't erase his name.

The fact is
The only work that really brings enjoyment
Is the kind that is for girl and boy meant.
Fall in love—you won't regret it.
That's the best work of all—if you can get it.

REFRAIN
Holding hands at midnight
'Neath a starry sky . . .
Nice work if you can get it,
And you can get it—if you try.

Strolling with the one girl,
Sighing sigh after sigh . . .
Nice work if you can get it,
And you can get it—if you try.

Just imagine someone
Waiting at the cottage door,
Where two hearts become one . . .
Who could ask for anything more?

Loving one who loves you,
And then taking that vow . . .
Nice work if you can get it,
And if you get it—Won't You Tell Me How?

Love Walked In

Nothing seemed to matter anymore;
Didn't care what I was headed for.
Time was standing still;
Nothing counted till
There came a knock-knock-knocking at the door.

Love walked right in
And drove the shadows away;
Love walked right in
And brought my sunniest day.

One magic moment,
And my heart seemed to know
That love said "Hello!"—
Though not a word was spoken.

One look, and I
Forgot the gloom of the past;
One look, and I
Had found my future at last.

One look, and I
Had found a world completely new,
When love walked in with you.

I Was Doing All Right

VERSE
Used to lead a quiet existence,
Always had my peace of mind.
Kept Old Man Trouble at a distance;
My days were silver-lined.

Right on top of the world I sat,
But look at me now—I don't know where I'm at.

REFRAIN
I was doing all right—
Nothing but rainbows in my sky;
I was doing all right
Till you came by.

Had no cause to complain—
Life was as sweet as apple pie;
Never noticed the rain
Till you came by.

But now, whenever you're away,
Can't sleep nights and suffer all the day.
I just sit and wonder
If love isn't one big blunder.

Still, when you hold me tight,
Tingling all through, I feel somehow
I was doing all right—
But I'm doing better than ever now!

Love Is Here to Stay

The more I read the papers,
The less I comprehend
The world and all its capers
And how it all will end.
Nothing seems to be lasting,
But that isn't our affair;
We've got something permanent—
I mean, in the way we care.

It's very clear
Our love is here to stay;
Not for a year,
But ever and a day.

The radio and the telephone
And the movies that we know
May just be passing fancies—
And in time may go.

But oh, my dear,
Our love is here to stay.
Together we're
Going a long, long way.

In time the Rockies may crumble,
Gibraltar may tumble
(They're only made of clay),
But—our love is here to stay.

I Love To Rhyme

There are men who, in their leisure,
Love to play the horses;
There are others who get pleasure
Cursing on golf courses.
General Grant loved to smoke;
Mark Twain loved to joke;
Radio comics love to pun—
But the thing I do is much more fun.

REFRAIN I
I love to rhyme—
Mountaineers love to climb—
Criminals love to crime—
But I love to rhyme.

What joy to croon:
Spoon, June, prune, moon, soon;
Chuckle, knuckle, nickel, fickle, pickle!
I love to rhyme.

Variety, society, propriety . . .
There's no stopping when you've begun;
Capacity, veracity, audacity . . .
Did you ever know such fun?

I love to rhyme—
And wouldn't it be sublime
If one day it could be
That *you* rhyme with *me*?

I love to rhyme—
Steeple bells love to chime—
Citrus fruit loves to lime—
But I love to rhyme.

Such pure delight—
Bite, sight, fight, quite, right;
Castle, tassel, muscle, tussle, Yussel!
I love to rhyme.

Algerian, Siberian, Shakespearean . . .
Tell me, how can you resist?
Amnesia, Rhodesia, Zambesia
Cannot lightly be dismissed.

I love to rhyme—
But here we are wasting time!
The day is overdue
When *I* rhyme with *you*!

By Strauss

Away with the music of Broadway!
Be off with your Irving Berlin!
Oh, I'd give no quarter
To Kern or Cole Porter,
And Gershwin keeps pounding on tin.
How can I be civil
When hearing this drivel?

It's only for nightclubbing souses.
Oh, give me the free'n'easy
Waltz that is Viennesey—
And, go tell the band
If they want a hand,
The waltz must be Strauss's.
Ya, ya, ya—
Give me Oom-pah-pah!

REFRAIN
When I want a melody
Lilting through the house,
Then I want a melody
By Strauss.
It laughs! It sings! The world is in rhyme,
Swinging to three-quarter time.
Let the Danube flow along,
And *The Fledermaus*!
Keep the wine and give me song
By Strauss.
By Jo, by Jing,
By Strauss is the thing!
So I say to Ha-cha-cha:
Heraus!
Just give me an Oom-pah-pah
By Strauss.

Tchaikowsky (and Other Russians)

VERSE (*not sung in original production*)

> Without the least excuse
> Or the slightest provocation,
> May I fondly introduce,
> For your mental delectation,
> The names that always give me brain
> concussion,
> The names of those composers known as
> Russian.

REFRAIN

> There's Malichevsky, Rubinstein,
> Arensky, and Tchaikowsky,
> Sapelnikoff, Dimitrieff, Tscherepnin,
> Kryjanowsky,
> Godowsky, Arteiboucheff, Moniuszko,
> Akimenko,
> Solovieff, Prokofieff, Tiomkin,
> Korestchenko.
>
> There's Glinka, Winkler, Bortniansky,
> Rebikoff, Ilyinsky;
> There's Medtner, Balakireff, Zolotareff,
> and Kvoschinsky.
> And Sokoloff and Kopyloff, Dukelsky,
> and Klenowsky,
> And Shostakovitsch, Borodine, Glière,
> and Nowakofski.

There's Liadoff and Karganoff,
    Markievitch, Pantschenko
And Dargomyzski, Stcherbatcheff,
    Scriabine, Vassilenko,
Stravinsky, Rimsky-Korsakoff,
    Mussorgsky, and Gretchaninoff
And Glazounoff and Caesar Cui,
    Kalinikoff, Rachmaninoff,

Stravinsky and Gretchaninoff,
Rumshinsky and Rachmaninoff,
I really have to stop, the subject has been
    dwelt
Upon enough!

ENSEMBLE: Stravinsky!
RINGMASTER: Gretchaninoff!
ENSEMBLE: Rumshinsky!
RINGMASTER: Rachmaninoff!
ENSEMBLE: He'd *better* stop because we feel we all
    have under-
Gone enough!

The Saga of Jenny

LIZA: There once was a girl named Jenny
        Whose virtues were varied and many—
        Excepting that she was inclined
        Always to make up her mind;
        And Jenny points a moral
        With which you cannot quarrel—
        As you will find.

ENSEMBLE: Who's Jenny?
        Never heard of Jenny!
        Jenny is out of place!

LIZA: But I am sure the court'll
        Find Jenny is immortal
        And has a bearing on this case!

JURY: As, for instance?
LIZA: Well, for instance—

REFRAIN

        Jenny made her mind up when she was
            three
        She, herself, was going to trim the
            Christmas tree.
        Christmas Eve she lit the candles—tossed
            the taper away.
        Little Jenny was an orphan on Christmas
            Day.

        Poor Jenny! Bright as a penny!
        Her equal would be hard to find.

She lost one dad and mother,
A sister and a brother—
But she would make up her mind.

JURY:　Little Jenny was an orphan on Christmas
　　　　Day.

LIZA:　Jenny made her mind up when she was
　　　　twelve
　　　　That into foreign languages she would
　　　　delve;
　　　　But at seventeen to Vassar it was quite a
　　　　blow
　　　　That in twenty-seven languages she
　　　　couldn't say no.

JURY:　Poor Jenny! Bright as a penny!
　　　　Her equal would be hard to find.

LIZA:　To Jenny I'm beholden.
　　　　Her heart was big and golden—
　　　　But she would make up her mind.

JURY:　In twenty-seven languages she couldn't
　　　　say no.

LIZA:　Jenny made her mind up at twenty-two
　　　　To get herself a husband was the thing to
　　　　do.
　　　　She got herself all dolled up in her satins
　　　　and furs
　　　　And she got herself a husband—but he
　　　　wasn't hers.

JURY:　Poor Jenny! Bright as a penny!
　　　　Her equal would be hard to find.

LIZA: Deserved a bed of roses
But history discloses
That she would make up her mind.

JURY: She got herself a husband—but he wasn't
hers.

LIZA: Jenny made her mind up at thirty-nine
She would take a trip to the Argentine.
She was only on vacation but the Latins
agree
Jenny was the one who started the Good
Neighbor Policy.

JURY: Poor Jenny! Bright as a penny!
Her equal would be hard to find.

LIZA: Oh, passion doesn't vanish
In Portuguese or Spanish—
But she would make up her mind.

JURY: She instituted the Good Neighbor Policy.

LIZA: Jenny made her mind up at fifty-one
She would write her memoirs before she
was done.
The very day her book was published,
hist'ry relates,
There were wives who shot their husbands
in some thirty-three states.

JURY: Poor Jenny! Bright as a penny!
Her equal would be hard to find.

LIZA: She could give cards and spade-ies
To many other ladies—
But she would make up her mind.

JURY: There were libel suits in forty of the
          forty-eight states.

LIZA: Jenny made her mind up at seventy-five
          She would live to be the oldest woman
             alive.
          But gin and rum and destiny play funny
             tricks,
          And poor Jenny kicked the bucket at
             seventy-six.

JURY: Jenny points a moral
          With which we cannot quarrel.
          Makes a lot of common sense!

LIZA: Jenny and her saga
          Prove that you are gaga
          If you don't keep sitting on the fence.

JURY: Jenny and her story
          Point the way to glory
          To all man and womankind.

ALL: Anyone with vision
          Comes to this decision:
          Don't make up—
          You shouldn't make up—
          You mustn't make up—
          Oh, never make up—
          Anyone with vision
          Comes to this decision:
          Don't make up your mind!

My Ship

My ship has sails that are made of silk—
The decks are trimmed with gold—
And of jam and spice
There's a paradise
In the hold.

My ship's aglow with a million pearls,
And rubies fill each bin;
The sun sits high
In a sapphire sky
When my ship comes in.

I can wait the years
Till it appears—
One fine day one spring.
But the pearls and such,
They won't mean much
If there's missing just one thing:

I do not care if that day arrives—
That dream need never be—
If the ship I sing
Doesn't also bring
My own true love to me—
If the ship I sing
Doesn't also bring
My own true love to me.

Midnight Music

Just a whisper, soft and low,
And midnight was aglow.
For oh, your words made midnight music—
Words that brought me such a thrill
The echoes haunt me still—
And always will.
In that midnight rendezvous
You said, "There's only you."
And oh, there never was such music!
Darkened streets began to shine
The moment midnight music made you mine.

Midnight shadows, dark and weird,
Completely disappeared
The moment we heard midnight music—
And no roaring of the "El,"
No taxi horn, no bell,
Could break the spell.
Through that midnight ballyhoo
You said, "There's only you!"
And oh, there never was such music!
Darkened streets began to shine
The moment midnight music made you mine.

Long Ago and Far Away

VERSE

Dreary days are over,
Life's a four-leaf clover.
Sessions of depressions are through:
Ev'ry hope I longed for long ago comes true.

REFRAIN

Long ago and far away
I dreamed a dream one day—
And now that dream is here beside me.
Long the skies were overcast,
But now the clouds have passed:
You're here at last!
Chills run up and down my spine,
Aladdin's lamp is mine:
The dream I dreamed was not denied me.
Just one look and then I knew
That all I longed for long ago was you.

The Duchess's Song—
"Sing Me Not a Ballad"

VERSE

I am not like Circe,
Who showed men no mercy;
Men are most important in my life.
Venus, Cleo, Psyche,

Are melodies in my key;
They knew how to live the high life.
Gallantry I find archaic,
Poetry I find prosaic.
Give me the man who's strong and silent:
Inarticulate—but vi'lent.

Sing me not a ballad,
Send me not a sonnet.
I require no ballad:
Rhyme and time are wasted on it.

Save your books and flowers;
They're not necessaries.
Oh, the precious hours
Lost in grim preliminaries!

Deck me not in jewels;
Sigh me not your sighs;
Duel me no duels;
And—please don't vocalize.

Romance me no romances;
Treasure not my glove.
Spare me your advances—
Just, oh just make love!
Spare me your advances—
Just, oh just make love!

Ode—"A Rhyme for Angela"

VERSE
It's always been a pleasure
To dedicate a measure
To the lady who intrigues me at the time.
Diana and Roxana
And Lana and Susannah
Were names I sang in rhythm and in rhyme.
Cornelia and Aurelia,
Cecelia and Ophelia,
Inspired lovely lyrics from my pen—
But Angela is something else again.

REFRAIN I
I can find a rhyme for Lucy—
For instance, her kiss is juicy.
But I must confess
I'm lost, more or less,
With Angela, Angela.

I can find a rhyme for Chloe—
For instance, her breast is snowy.
But rhyming is lame
When you get a name
Like Angela, Angela.

If only her name were Olivia,
She could be a cute bit of trivia;
If she were tagged Maria,
Or even Dorothea,
She'd be my Sole Mia
Divine.

I can find a rhyme for Irma:
She's Heaven on Terra Firma.
But Angela has no patter—
And yet, what does it matter
If Angela's heart rhymes with mine!

I can find a rhyme for Margot:
On her favors there's no embargo.
But rhyming is tough
When one's bit of fluff
Is Angela, Angela.

What a joy to rhyme Amanda:
Each movement is pure propaganda.
(The heights I can climb—
Till I seek a rhyme
For Angela, Angela.)

If only her name were Titania,
I'd star her in my miscellanea;
If she were called Marcella
Or even Isabella
This most poetic fella
Could shine.

I can find a rhyme for Edith
She possesses what Everyman needeth.
But Angela has no patter—
And yet, what does it matter
If Angela's heart rhymes with mine!

There's Nothing Like Marriage for People

VERSE I

Imagine living with someone
Who's longing to live with you!

Imagine signing a lease together
And hanging a Matisse together!

Oh, what felicity
In domesticity!

Let no one disparage
Marriage!

Being alone and breaking bread together—
Reading *The New Yorker* in bed together.

What else are we living for?

Growing old together—
Sharing a cold together—
Starting a family tree together—
Voting for the G.O.P. together—

REFRAIN I

There's nothing, oh nothing, like marriage for people—
It means you're living at last!
Carry me over the threshold!
When you her flesh hold,
On life you get a fresh hold.
How can we miss? There'll be bliss unsurpassed!
Give me the kingdom
Of wedding ringdom!

Let there be ding-a-dong up there in the steeple
And thousands of old shoes to throw!
There's nothing as wonderful as marriage for people
And we are the people who know!

Imagine signing a license
And finally settling down.

Of music growing fond together,
Sleeping through *Pelléas and Mélisande* together.

No more philandering
When on my hand a ring.

Oh, living is lifeless
Wifeless!

Palm Beach in the very late fall together—
Getting coats of tan in the altogether—

What more can life hold in store?

Shopping at Cartier's together—
Giving dinner partiers together—

Finishing a magnum of Lanson together—
Making application at Groton for our gran'son
        together—

There's nothing, oh nothing, like marriage for people.
It means you're living at last!
Hurry, let's call up the minister!
Why be a sinister

Old bachelor or spinister?
Give me the feast, not the fast of the past.
If there's misogyny
You can't have progeny.
Let there be ding-a-dong up there in the steeple
And heaven on earth here below;
There's nothing as wonderful as marriage for people—
And we are the people who know.

The Land of Opportunitee

INTRODUCTION

All the immigrants came to the U.S.A.
Because they had been told
That in ev'ry cit*ee* of the U.S.A.
The streets were paved with gold.

They dug themselves a pile,
Then went back to Italy and the Emerald Isle.

In the U.S.A. not all the gold is gone—
The pioneer spirit will carry on.

For example and to wit—
We give you a sample of it:

VERSE I

You take the subway to the street called Wall;
On a dignified broker's man you call.
He shows you a ticker goes tick, tick, tick—
And helps you a stock to pick pick, pick.

Fascinating names you have from which to choose
Biggest corporations which cannot lose:
Delaware and Lackawanna,
United Fruit and Banana—
Or you buy Nash Kelvinator,
Maybe Otis Elevator.
Oh boy, can't miss!
Anaconda Copper Mining,
'Merican Smelting and Refining;
Biggest bargains ever wuz,
Like Paramount and Warner Bros.
Oh boy, some class!
With a thousand corporations to pick from—
You clean up, my friend, or else you're dumb.

REFRAIN I
You buy a block of stock, say, American Tel;
Goes up a hundred points, then quickly you sell.
Making a fortune is A B C,
In the Grand Land of Opportunitee.
Making a fortune is A B C,
In the Grand Land of Opportunitee.
It's so simple, anyone can do it.
Just open an account and nothing to it.

VERSE 2
By now you have piled up such a bundle of jack
You take a taxi to the nearest racetrack.
Is easy to take the racetrack by storm—
A pencil, a program, a "Racing Form."

Then you handicap the possibilities
By the Past Performances of all the gee-gees:
Man-o'-War, Sun Beau, and Stymie—
They have not done badly by me.
Good-bye, Care!—and also, Trouble!
(Compliments of Daily Double)
Oh boy, some tips!
In the first, I like Disraeli;
In the second race, Rose Bailey.
In the big race, Tom the Peeper—
(Looks to me like he's a sleeper.)
Oh boy, sure things!
So you study and study all the dope you got,
And at the window you bet a long *shot*.

REFRAIN 2

They're at the gate—and off! The race she is run.
Your horse comes in and pays a hundred to one.
Making a fortune is A B C,
In the Grand Land of Opportunitee.
Making a fortune is A B C,
In the Grand Land of Opportunitee.
It's so simple, anyone can do it.
Take a taxi to the racetrack—nothing to it.

VERSE 3

Though now you have got of money quite a store,
After all you're only human, so you want more.
So you go to a radio show which is
A question-and-answer program known as quiz.

When you face the mike you make no faux pas;
All night long you studied the Britanni*ca*:
What's the color of red roses?
On your feet how many toes is?
Name the month after September.
What's on Twenty-fifth December?
Oh boy, oh boy!
In one day how many hours?
Oranges are fruits or flowers?
Which is more, ten or eleven?
Just what year was Nineteen-Seven?
Oh boy, quiz kid!
Your answers have put the man in his place,
But now the big moment you must face.

REFRAIN 3
The questioner he ask you, "What is your name?"
You get a hundred thousand dollars if you tell him the
    same.
Making a fortune is A B C,
In the Grand Land of Opportunitee.
And—
If you know what flag is Red, White, and Blue,
He will throw in the sponsor's daughter too.
Making a fortune is A B C,
In the Grand Land of Opportunitee.
It's so simple, anyone can do it.
Just visit a quiz program—nothing to it!

You buy a block of stock, American Tel;
Goes up a hundred points, then quickly you sell.
They're at the gate—they're off! The race she is run.
Your horse comes in and pays a hundred to one.
The questioner he ask you, "What is your name?"
You get a hundred thousand dollars if you tell him the
    same.
Making a fortune is A B C,
In the Grand Land of Opportunitee!

Good-Bye to All That

VERSE

NED: Don't look now, but summer's over;
    The North Wind is here.
    The red rose, the four-leaf clover,
    Disappear.

    The shadows start to fall;
    The writing's on the wall.
    You can't, you can't fight City Hall.

REFRAIN I

MADGE: The things we planned—
    Good-bye to all that!
    We built on sand—
    Good-bye to all that!

    Whoever called a parting sweet sorrow
    Never knew
    What I'm going through.

The years ahead
We never will share;
Our golden anniversary
Melts into thin air.
The paradise we could have known tomorrow,
Good-bye, good-bye to all that!

REFRAIN 2

NED: Those gay hellos—
Good-bye to all that!
The book we close—
Good-bye to all that!

Why do they call a parting sweet sorrow?
This farewell
Is hurting like hell.

MADGE: So long, my own,
Can't blame you at all.
NED: Our bright and sunny future
We'll never recall.
MADGE: The years for which I'd steal or beg or
borrow . . .
BOTH: Good-bye, good-bye to all that.

INTERLUDE

NED: If you and I and love weren't in a spin,
What a world this old world might have been!
Up on a rainbow we would find us,
All of our lonesome nights behind us.
MADGE: You were about to take me to far-off places.
We were about to meet new friends and faces.

Oh, what a lovely picture you had painted!
Off in a world where we could really get
    acquainted!

NED: This moment is the one I've been living for:
Being one with the one I adore.

REPEAT REFRAIN 2

Changing My Tune

VERSE

Yesterday the sky was black
And I was blue.
Yesterday—Alas, alack!—
I thought I was through.
But knock on wood!
My job looks good,
And having found a dwelling,
My happiness is beyond the telling.

REFRAIN 1

Castles were crumbling
And daydreams were tumbling—
December was battling with June—
But on this bright afternoon
Guess I'll be changing my tune.

Kept on despairing,
Beyond any caring

If I jumped out of a balloon—
But I'm arranging
From now to be changing my tune.

At last the skies are bright and shiny;
It's a human world once more.
Yesterday's troubles are tiny—
What was I worried for?

Wanted a permit
To make me a hermit,
To grumble and glare at the moon—
But I'm arranging
From now to be changing my tune.

REFRAIN 2
No more the feeling
That my world is reeling—
No fearing I'll fall in a swoon.
Problems are all picayune—
That's why I'm changing my tune.

Felt like a sailor
Adrift on a whaler
A-sailing into a typhoon—
But I'm arranging
From now to be changing my tune.

At last the skies are bright and shiny;
It's a human world once more.
Yesterday's troubles are tiny—
What was I worried for?

No more resentment,
I'm full of contentment—
Afloat on a dreamy lagoon;
And I'm arranging
From now to be changing my tune.

Aren't You Kind of Glad We Did?

VERSE

JOHN: Oh, it really wasn't my intention
To disregard convention;
It was just an impulse that had to be obeyed.

Beacon Hill behavior we've been scorning,
CYNTHIA: But I'll not go in mourning—
Though my reputation is blemished, I'm
afraid.

What's done, is done.
JOHN: But wasn't—and isn't—it fun?

REFRAIN I

Honestly, I thought you wouldn't;
Naturally, you thought you couldn't.
And probably we shouldn't—
But aren't you kind of glad we did?
Actually, it all was blameless;
Nevertheless, they'll call it shameless.
So the lady shall be nameless,
But aren't you kind of glad we did?

CYNTHIA: Socially, I'll be an outcast:
Obviously we dined alone.
On my good name there will be doubt cast—
With never a sign of any chaperone.

JOHN: No matter how they may construe it—
Whether or not we have to rue it—
Whatever made us do it—
Say, aren't you kind of glad we did?

REFRAIN 2

CYNTHIA: Honestly, I thought I wouldn't;
Naturally, I thought I couldn't.
And probably I shouldn't—

JOHN: But aren't you kind of glad we did?
The community will call me viper.

CYNTHIA: The opportunity should have been riper.

BOTH: We'll have to pay the piper—
But what we did we're glad we did.

CYNTHIA: Supper was quite above suspicion;
Milk in the glasses when they'd clink.

JOHN: Listening to a tired musician—

CYNTHIA: But what is it Mrs. Grundy's going to think?

JOHN: I'm a rounder, a bounder, a cad, a Boston
blighter—

CYNTHIA: You shouldn't be seen alone with your
typewriter.

BOTH: Let's turn to something brighter:
Whatever we did, we're glad we did.

The Back Bay Polka

REFRAIN 1
Give up the fond embrace,
Pass up that pretty face;
You're of the human race—
But not in Boston.

Think as your neighbors think,
Make lemonade your drink;
You'll be the Missing Link—
If you don't wear spats in Boston.

Painters who paint the nude
We keep repressing.
We take the attitude
Even a salad must have dressing.

New York or Philadelph'
Won't put you on the shelf
If you would be yourself—
But you can't be yourself in Boston.

You can't be yourself,
You can't be yourself,
You can't be yourself in Boston.

REFRAIN 2
Don't speak the naked truth—
What's naked is uncouth;
It may go in Duluth—
But not in Boston.

Keep up the cultured pose;
Keep looking down your nose;
Keep up the status quos—
Or they keep you out of Boston.

Books that are out of key
We quickly bury;
You will find liberty
In Mr. Webster's dictionary.

Laughter goes up the flue;
Life is one big taboo;
No matter what you do—
It isn't being done in Boston.

It isn't being done,
It isn't being done,
It isn't being done in Boston.

REFRAIN 3
Somewhere the fairer sex
Has curves that are convex,
And girls don't all wear "specs"—
But not in Boston.

One day it's much too hot,
Then cold as you-know-what;
In all the world there's not
Weather anywhere like Boston.

At natural history
We are colossal.
That is because, you see,
At first hand we study the fossil.

Strangers are all dismissed—
(Not that we're prejudiced)
You simply don't exist—
If you haven't been born in Boston.

You haven't been born,
You haven't been born,
If you haven't been born in Boston.

REFRAIN 4
On Boston beans you dine,
Then go to bed at nine.
You mustn't undermine
The town of Boston.

No song except a hymn—
And keep your language prim:
You call a leg a "limb"
Or they boot you out of Boston.

You're of the bourgeoisie
And no one bothers—
Not if your fam'ly tree
Doesn't date from the Pilgrim Fathers.

Therefore, when all is said,
Life is so limited,
You find, unless you're dead,
You never get ahead in Boston.

You never get ahead,
You never get ahead,
You never get ahead in Boston.

Shoes With Wings On

VERSE

Aladdin had a wonderful lamp;
King Midas had the touch of gold;
In magic they had many a champ
'Way back in days of old.
But magic was in its infancy;
Today they'd ring no bell.
Today they'd mimic
Me and my gimmick
To cast a spell.

REFRAIN

When I've got shoes with wings on—
The winter's gone, the spring's on.
When I've got shoes with wings on—
The town is full of rhythm and the world's in rhyme.

The Neon City glows up;
My pretty Pretty shows up.
We'll dance until they close up—
(Got my Guardian Angel working overtime.)

I give Aladdin the lamp,
Midas the gold.
Who needs a wizard or magician
In the old tradition?
That's not competition—
I've got 'em beat a thousandfold!
Why?

'Cause I've got shoes with wings on—
And living has no strings on.
I put those magic things on,
And I go flying with 'em—
And the town is full of rhythm
And the world's in rhyme.

TAG

Happens ev'ry time;
Put my shoes with wings on—
Yes, siree! The world's in rhyme!

Manhattan Downbeat

VERSE

From Battery Park to Spuyten Duyvil
In the time when Peter Stuyvesant held sway,
For peacefulness this island had no rival—
But it's just a little bit different today.

If you should ask if I've nostalgic yearning
For the charm and quaintness of the long ago,
And would—if I could—to those days be returning,
The answer, emphatically, is "No!"

REFRAIN

Just give me that Manhattan Downbeat
That beats a tempo of its own!
You've got to shout, "This *is* it!"
The day you visit
The jumpin'est town was ever known.

Keep your Paree and London Town Beat;
Pop Knickerbocker stands alone.
Drive up any avenue,
Swing down any street—
There's no beat has Manhattan Downbeat beat!

PATTER

Listen to that bebop orchestration
In a symphony of cosmic sound!
Taxi horns and tintinnabulation . . .
Planes above and subways underground . . .
Glamour, glitter—
Sweet and bitter—
How you laugh and cry!
Faster, faster,
To disaster
Or a goal up high!
Listen to those seven million voices!
The Tower of Babel merely was a toot!
Listen—and your beating heart rejoices,
Getting that electrifying boot!
Right from the minute
You get in it,
Got to follow suit!

TAG

Keep your Paree and London Town Beat;
Pop Knickerbocker stands alone.
Drive up any avenue,
Swing down any street—
There's no beat has Manhattan Downbeat beat!

There's no beat has Manhattan Downbeat beat!
Battery Park to Spuyten Duyvil,
Manhattan has no rival—
No beat has Manhattan Downbeat beat!

There Is No Music

REFRAIN
Stars without glitter,
Sun without gold;
Nightfall is bitter,
Endless, and cold.
Silent the city,
Silent the sea—
There is no music for me.

Gone the charms
Of his arms,
Gone the spell that dispelled all alarms.
Gone the bright,
Twinkling light
That beguiled
As he smiled
And enfolded me tight.

Gone is the singer,
Lost is the song
That I longed for all my life long.

Once there was music,
Joyous and free;
Now salty tears glisten;
All night I listen,
But there's no music for me.

In Our United State

VERSE
The state of the world is such
That the world is in quite a state.
But let's not worry too much;
Let the rest of the world debate.
Right now the thing to discuss
Is the wonderful status of us.

REFRAIN I
The state of our union,
Hearts in communion,
Never will know any foreign entanglements;
Outsiders will not rate
In our united state!

We'll make the altar
Strong as Gibraltar—
Fooling around will be unconstitutional.
Great will be our united state!

With nothing but true love in the ascendance,
We'll always sign and renew

A Declaration of Dependence—
Where you depend on me
And I depend on you.

Peaceful and cozy,
We'll have a rosy
Future with a House of cute Representatives;
So, I can hardly wait,
Darling, for our united state!

Our annual budget?
I'll let you judge it—
You do what you will with what's in our treasury;
I won't investigate
In our united state.

This is my platform:
That face and that form!
You will find out that's a permanent policy
Slated for our united state.

But there will be changes I'll be unfolding:
Withholding taxes are through—
For when it's you, dear, that I'm holding,
You can't withhold on me—
I can't withhold on you.

We'll have a White House,
Small, but a bright house,
Built on the Pursuit of Star-Spangled Happiness.
Hurry, let's name the date,
Darling, for our united state!

Applause, Applause

VERSE

When the voodoo drum is drumming
Or the hummingbird is humming,
Does it thrill you? Does it fill you with delight?
To continue with our jingle:
Are you one of those who tingle
To your shoes-ies at the blues-ies in the night?
Oh, the sounds of bugles calling
Or Niag'ra Falls a-falling
May enchant you—We will grant you that they might;
But for us on the stage, oh brother!
There's just one sound and no other:

REFRAIN I
Applause, applause!
We like applause because
It means when it is striking us
The audience is liking us.

Our work demands
You don't sit on your hands—
And if the hand's tremendous,
You send us!

We live, we thrive,
You keep us all alive
With "*Bravo!*" and "*Bravissimo!*"
We're dead if it's *pianissimo*.

Our quirk is work,
Is work we never shirk

In a happyland of tinsel and gauze,
Because—we like applause!

Whether you're a Swiss bell ringer
Or a crooner or a singer
Or monologist, ventriloquist, or what—
Or a dog act or magician
Or a musical-saw musician
Or an ingenue or pianist who is hot—
Whether you play Punchinello,
Little Eva, or Othello—
Having heard the call, you've given all you've got.
And what better reward for a trouper
Than the sound we consider super?

Applause, applause!
Vociferous applause
From orchestra to gallery
Could mean a raise in salary.

Give out, give in!—
Be noisy, make a din!
(The manager, he audits
Our plaudits.)

We won renown
When opening out of town;
(In Boston and in Rockaway
They heard applause a block away)—

If we've come through,
Give credit where it's due,
And obey the theatre's unwritten laws,
Because—we like applause!

Gotta Have Me Go with You

VERSE

What a spot, this—
Not so hot, this!
Hey, there—shy one,
Come be my one!
Please don't rush off—
Want no brush-off.
I can't compel you
To buy what I'd sell you . . .
But I've got to tell you
Like so:

REFRAIN

You wanna have bells that'll ring?
You wanna have songs that'll sing?
You want your sky a baby blue?
You gotta have me go with you!

Hey, you fool, you—
Why so cool, you,
When I'm ready
To go steady?

You wanna have eyes that'll shine?
You wanna have grapes on the vine?
You want a love that's truly true?
You gotta have me go with you!

Why the holdout?
Have you sold out?
Time you woke up,
Time you spoke up!

This line I'm handing you is not a handout;
As a team we'd be a standout.

You wanna live high on a dime?
You wanna have two hearts in rhyme?
Gotta have me go with you all the time!

It's a New World

Original Version

VERSE
How wonderful that I'm beholding
A Never-Never Land unfolding—
Where we polish up the stars
And mountains we move
In a life where all the pleasures
We will prove.

REFRAIN
It's a new world I see—
A new world for me!

The tears have rolled off my cheek,
And fears fade away ev'ry time you speak . . .

A new world, though we're in a tiny room—'
What a vision of joy and blossom and bloom!

A newfound promise, one that will last—
So I'm holding on and I'm holding fast!

You've brought a new world to me,
And that it'll always, always be!

1963 Version

VERSE

How wonderful that I'm beholding
A vision of a world unfolding—
Where we reach up to the stars
As mountains we move
In a life where all the pleasures
We will prove.

REFRAIN

It's a new world I see—
A new world for me!

The tears have rolled off my cheek,
And fears fade away, seeing all I seek:

A new world—though it once was just a dream—
Full of love, full of faith and self-esteem.

A newfound promise, one that will last—
So I'm holding on and I'm holding fast!

Hope brings a new world to me;
Let's hope it's a world that'll always be!

The Man That Got Away

The night is bitter,
The stars have lost their glitter;
The winds grow colder
And suddenly you're older—
And all because of the man that got away.

No more his eager call,
The writing's on the wall;
The dreams you've dreamed have all
Gone astray.

The man that won you
Has run off and undone you.
That great beginning
Has seen the final inning.
Don't know what happened. It's all a crazy game.

No more that all-time thrill,
For you've been through the mill—
And never a new love will
Be the same.

Good riddance, good-bye!
Ev'ry trick of his you're on to.
But, fools will be fools—
And where's he gone to?

The road gets rougher,
It's lonelier and tougher.
With hope you burn up—
Tomorrow he may turn up.
There's just no letup the livelong night and day.

Ever since this world began
There is nothing sadder than
A one-man woman looking for
The man that got away . . .
The man that got away.

BIOGRAPHICAL NOTE

COPYRIGHT & PUBLICATION
INFORMATION

INDEX OF TITLES

BIOGRAPHICAL NOTE

Ira Gershwin was born December 6, 1896, in New York City. His first stage success came with his lyrics (written under the pseudonym Arthur Francis) for Vincent Youmans' score for the 1921 musical *Two Little Girls in Blue*. His long collaboration with his brother George hit its stride with *Lady, Be Good!* in 1924, followed by works that included *Oh, Kay!*, *Strike Up the Band*, *Girl Crazy*, *Of Thee I Sing* (for which he shared a Pulitzer Prize with George S. Kaufman and Morrie Ryskind), and *Porgy and Bess* (with DuBose and Dorothy Heyward). In 1936 the Gershwins went to Hollywood where they collaborated on the films *Shall We Dance*, *A Damsel in Distress*, and *The Goldwyn Follies*. After George's death in 1937, Ira went on to collaborate on films, Broadway shows, and individual songs with other songwriters including Harold Arlen, Aaron Copland, Vernon Duke, Jerome Kern, Burton Lane, Arthur Schwartz, Harry Warren, and Kurt Weill. His book *Lyrics on Several Occasions* was published in 1959. Ira Gershwin died on August 17, 1983, at his home in Beverly Hills, California, where he had lived with his wife, Leonore Strunsky Gershwin, for over 40 years.

COPYRIGHT AND
PUBLICATION INFORMATION

The texts in this volume are taken from *The Complete Lyrics of Ira Gershwin*, edited by Robert Kimball (New York: Knopf, 1993). For all song copyrights: All rights reserved. International copyright secured. Used by permission.

The following copyright information should be added to individual notices according to the corresponding numbers:

7. © (Renewed) Harms, Inc., assigned to WB Music Corp. for the United States; Chappell & Co. and New World Music Company (Ltd.) administered by WB Music Corp. for all British Reversionary Territories; New World Music Company (Ltd.) administered by WB Music Corp. for all other countries.

8. © (Renewed) New World Music Corp. assigned to WB Music Corp. for the United States; Chappell & Co. and New World Music Company (Ltd.) administered by WB Music Corp. for all British Reversionary Territories; New World Music Company (Ltd.) administered by WB Music Corp. for all other countries.

9. © Ira Gershwin Music administered by WB Music Corp. and Gilbert Keyes Music for the United States and all other countries.

10. © (Renewed) New World Music Corp. assigned to WB Music Corp. for the United States; Chappell & Co. and New World Music Company (Ltd.) administered by WB Music Corp. for all British Reversionary Territories; New World Music Company (Ltd.) administered by WB Music Corp., for all other countries. Additional material © George Gershwin Music and Ira Gershwin Music both administered by Warner Bros. Music. For the United States and all other countries.

11. © (Renewed) Gershwin Publishing Corp. (Renewed) by Chappell & Co, assigned to George Gershwin Music, Ira Gershwin Music, and DuBose and Dorothy Heyward Memorial Fund Publishing (all administered by WB Music Corp.) for the United States; Chappell & Co. for all other countries.

12. © (Renewed) Chappell & Co. assigned to Chappell & Co. and Ira Gershwin Music administered by WB Music Corp. for the United States; Chappell & Co. for all other countries.

13. © (Renewed) Gershwin Publishing Corp. administered by Chappell & Co. assigned to George Gershwin Music and Ira Gershwin Music, both administered by WB Music Corp. for the United States; Chappell & Co. for all other countries.

14. © (Renewed) Chappell & Co. assigned to George Gershwin Music and Ira Gershwin Music, both administered by WB Music Corp. for the United States; Chappell & Co. for all other countries.

15. © (Renewed) Jerome Kern and Ira Gershwin assigned to T. B. Harms, Inc., administered by PolyGram International Publishing as successor-in-interest for the United States and all other countries.

16. © (Renewed) Chappell & Co. assigned to Chappell & Co. and Hampshire House Publishing Corp. for the United States; Chappell & Co. for all other countries.

17. © (Renewed) Putnam Music, Inc., administered by Polygram International Publishing, Inc., as successor-in-interest for the United States and all other countries.

18. © (renewed) Gershwin Publishing Corp. assigned to Chappell & Co. for the United States and all other countries.

19. © (Renewed) Harry Warren Music and Loews, Inc., assigned to Chappell & Co. and Four Jays Music Company for the United States and all other countries.

20. © (Renewed) Loews, Inc., assigned to Ira Gershwin Music administered by WB Music Corp. and Four Jays Music Company for the United States; Chappell & Co. and Four Jays Music Company for all other countries.

21. © (Renewed) Loews, Inc., assigned to Ira Gershwin Music administered by WB Music Corp. and Chappell & Co. for the United States and all other countries.

22. © (Renewed) Loews, Inc., assigned to EMI Feist Catalog Inc., as successor-in-interest for the United States and all other countries.

23. © (Renewed) Harwin Music Co. assigned to Harwin Music Co. administered by MPL Communications and New World Music Company (Ltd.) administered by WB Music Corp. for the United States; Harwin Music Co. administered by MPL Communications for all other countries.

24. © New World Music Corp. assigned to George Gershwin Music and Ira Gershwin Music both administered by WB Music Corp. for the United States and all other countries.

You May Throw All the Rice You Desire. Written in 1917. © 1973, 1993 Ira Gershwin Music.[1]

The Real American Folk Song (Is A Rag). From *Ladies First* (1918). © 1959 (Renewed) Chappell & Co.[2]

I'm Tickled Silly. From *Two Little Girls in Blue* (1921). Lyric © 1993 Ira Gershwin Music.[1]

Mischa, Jascha, Toscha, Sascha. Written in 1922.

Fascinating Rhythm. From *Lady, Be Good!* (1924) © 1924 (Renewed) WB Music Corp.[7]

The Half of It Dearie, Blues. From *Lady, Be Good!* (1924) © 1924 (Renewed) WB Music Corp.7

Little Jazz Bird. From *Lady, Be Good!* (1924) © 1924 (Renewed) WB Music Corp.[7]

The Man I Love. From *Lady, Be Good!* (1924) © 1924 (Renewed) WB Music Corp.[7]

These Charming People. From *Tip-Toes* (1925) © 1925 (Renewed) WB Music Corp.[3]

Sweet and Lowdown. From *Tip-Toes* (1925) © 1925 (Renewed) WB Music Corp.[7]

Gather Ye Rosebuds. From *Tip-Toes* (1925) © 1987 George Gershwin Music and Ira Gershwin Music.[6]

Sunny Disposish. From *Americana* (1926) © 1926 (Renewed) WB Music Corp. and Warner Bros. Inc.[4]

Do, Do, Do. From *Oh, Kay!* (1926) © 1926 (Renewed) WB Music Corp.[7]

Someone to Watch Over Me. From *Oh, Kay!* (1926) © 1926 (Renewed) WB Music Corp.[7]

Strike Up The Band. From *Strike Up the Band* (1927 and 1930) © 1927 (Renewed) WB Music Corp.[8]

'S Wonderful. From *Funny Face* (1927) © 1927 (Renewed) WB Music Corp.[8]

My One and Only. From *Funny Face* (1927) © 1927 (Renewed) WB Music Corp.[8]

The Babbitt and the Bromide. From *Funny Face* (1927) © 1927 (Renewed) WB Music Corp.[8]

The World Is Mine. From *Funny Face* (1927) © 1927 (Renewed) WB Music Corp.[8]

How Long Has This Been Going On? From *Funny Face* (1927) and *Rosalie* (1928) © 1927 (Renewed) WB Music Corp.[8]

New York Serenade. From *Rosalie* (1928) © 1977 George Gershwin Music and Ira Gershwin Music.[5]

I've Got a Crush on You. From *Treasure Girl* (1928) and *Strike Up the Band* (1930) © 1930 (Renewed) WB Music Corp.[8]

I Don't Think I'll Fall in Love Today. From *Treasure Girl* (1928) © 1928 (Renewed) WB Music Corp.[8]

What Causes That? From *Treasure Girl* (1928) © 1987 George Gershwin and Ira Gershwin Music.[24]

Home Blues. From *Show Girl* (1929) © 1990, 1993 Ira Gershwin Music and Gilbert Keyes Music.[9]

Soon. From *Strike Up the Band* (1930) © 1929 (Renewed) WB Music Corp.[8]

Bidin' My Time. From *Girl Crazy* (1930) © 1930 (Renewed) WB Music Corp.[8]

Could You Use Me? From *Girl Crazy* (1930) © 1930 (Renewed) WB Music Corp.[8]

Embraceable You. From *Girl Crazy* (1930) © 1930 (Renewed) WB Music Corp.[8]

Sam and Delilah. From *Girl Crazy* (1930) © 1930 (Renewed) WB Music Corp.[8]

I Got Rhythm. From *Girl Crazy* (1930) © 1930 (Renewed) WB Music Corp.[8]

But Not for Me. From *Girl Crazy* (1930) © 1930 (Renewed) WB Music Corp.[8]

Delishious. From *Delicious* (1931) © 1931 (Renewed) WB Music Corp.[8]

Love Is Sweeping the Country. From *Of Thee I Sing* (1931) © 1931 (Renewed) WB Music Corp.[8]

Of Thee I Sing. From *Of Thee I Sing* (1931) © 1931 (Renewed) WB Music Corp.[8]

Who Cares? From *Of Thee I Sing* (1931) © 1931 (Renewed) WB Music Corp.[8]

I've Got to Be There. From *Pardon My English* (1933) © 1933 (Renewed) WB Music Corp.[8]

Isn't It a Pity? From *Pardon My English* (1933) © 1932 (Renewed) WB Music Corp.[8]

Freud and Jung and Adler. From *Pardon My English* (1933) © 1993 George Gershwin Music and Ira Gershwin Music.[5]

Union Square and Down with Everyone Who's Up. From *Let 'Em Eat Cake* (1933) © 1933 (Renewed) WB Music Corp. Additional material © 1987 George Gershwin and Ira Gershwin Music.[10]

Mine. From *Let 'Em Eat Cake* (1933) © 1933 (Renewed) WB Music Corp.[8]

It Ain't Necessarily So. From *Porgy and Bess* (1935) © 1935 (Renewed) George Gershwin Music, Ira Gershwin Music and DuBose and Dorothy Heyward Memorial Fund Publishing.[11]

Island in the West Indies. From *Ziegfeld Follies of 1936* © 1935 (Renewed) Chappell & Co. and Ira Gershwin Music.[12]

The Economic Situation. From *Ziegfeld Follies of 1936* © 1993 Ira Gershwin Music.[11]

I Can't Get Started. From *Ziegfeld Follies of 1936* © 1935 (Renewed) Chappell & Co., and Ira Gershwin Music.[12]

(I've Got) Beginner's Luck. From *Shall We Dance* (1937) © 1936 (Renewed) George Gershwin Music and Ira Gershwin Music.[13]

They All Laughed. From *Shall We Dance* (1937) © 1936 (Renewed) George Gershwin Music and Ira Gershwin Music.[13]

They Can't Take That Away from Me. From *Shall We Dance* (1937) © 1936 (Renewed) George Gershwin Music and Ira Gershwin Music.[13]

Let's Call the Whole Thing Off. From *Shall We Dance* (1937) ©1936 (Renewed) George Gershwin Music and Ira Gershwin Music.[13]

I Can't Be Bothered Now. From *A Damsel in Distress* (1937) © 1937 (Renewed) George Gershwin Music and Ira Gershwin Music.[13]

Things Are Looking Up. From *A Damsel in Distress* (1937) © 1937 (Renewed) George Gershwin Music and Ira Gershwin Music.[13]

A Foggy Day (in London Town). From *A Damsel in Distress* (1937) © 1937 (Renewed) George Gershwin Music and Ira Gershwin Music.[13]

Nice Work If You Can Get It. From *A Damsel in Distress* (1937) © 1937 (Renewed) George Gershwin Music and Ira Gershwin Music.[13]

Love Walked In. From *The Goldwyn Follies* (1938) © 1937 (Renewed) George Gershwin Music and Ira Gershwin Music.[13]

I Was Doing All Right. From *The Goldwyn Follies* (1938) © 1937 (Renewed) George Gershwin Music and Ira Gershwin Music.[13]

Love Is Here to Stay. From *The Goldwyn Follies* (1938) © 1937, 1938 (Renewed) George Gershwin Music and Ira Gershwin Music.[13]

I Love to Rhyme. From *The Goldwyn Follies* (1938) © 1937 (Renewed) George Gershwin Music and Ira Gershwin Music.[13]

By Strauss. From *The Show Is On* (1936) © 1936 (Renewed) George Gershwin Music and Ira Gershwin Music.[14]

Tchaikowsky (And Other Russians) From *Lady in the Dark* (1941) © 1941 (Renewed) Chappell & Co. and Hampshire House Publishing Corp.[16]

The Saga of Jenny. From *Lady in the Dark* (1941) © 1941 (Renewed) Chappell & Co, and Hampshire House Publishing Corp.[16]

My Ship. From *Lady in the Dark* (1941) © 1941 (Renewed) Chappell & Co. and Hampshire House Publishing Corp.[16]

Midnight Music. From *Cover Girl* (1944) © 1943 (Renewed) PolyGram International Publishing Inc.[15]

Long Ago (and Far Away). From *Cover Girl* (1944) © 1944 (Renewed) Poly-Gram International Publishing, Inc.[15]

The Duchess's Song—"Sing Me Not a Ballad". From *The Firebrand of Florence* (1945) ©1945 (Renewed) Chappell & Co. and Hampshire House Publishing Corp.[16]

Ode—"A Rhyme for Angela". From *The Firebrand of Florence* (1945) © 1945 (Renewed) Chappell & Co. and Hampshire House Publishing Corp.[16]

There's Nothing Like Marriage for People. From *Park Avenue* (1946) ©1959 (Renewed) Ira Gershwin; © 1993 Ira Gershwin Music.[1]

The Land of Opportunitee. From *Park Avenue* (1946) © 1959 Ira Gershwin. ©1993 Ira Gerswein Music.[17]

Good-Bye to All That. From *Park Avenue* (1946) © 1946 (Renewed) Poly-Gram International Publishing, Inc.[17]

Changing My Tune. From *The Shocking Miss Pilgrim* (1947) © 1946 (Renewed) Chappell & Co.[18]

Aren't You Kind of Glad We Did? From *The Shocking Miss Pilgrim* (1946) © (Renewed) Chappell & Co.[18]

The Back Bay Polka. From *The Shocking Miss Pilgrim* (1947) © 1946 (Renewed) Chappell & Co.[18]

Shoes with Wings On. From *The Barkleys of Broadway* (1949) © 1948, 1949 (Renewed) Chappell & Co. and Four Jays Music Company.[19]

Manhattan Downbeat. From *The Barkleys of Broadway* (1949) © 1948 (Renewed) Ira Gershwin Music and Four Jays Music Company.[20]

There Is No Music. From *The Barkleys of Broadway* (1949) © 1948 (Renewed) Ira Gershwin Music and Four Jays Music Company.[20]

In Our United State. From *Give a Girl a Break* (1953) © 1951, 1953 (Renewed) EMI Feist Catalog Inc.[22]

Applause, Applause. From *Give a Girl a Break* 1953 © 1952 (Renewed) Ira Gershwin Music and Chappell & Co.[21]

Gotta Have Me Go with You. From *A Star is Born* (1954) © 1954 (Renewed) Harwin Music Corp. and New World Music Company (Ltd.).[23]

It's a New World. From *A Star Is Born* (1954) © 1954 (Renewed) Harwin Music Corp. and New World Music Company (Ltd.).[23]

The Man That Got Away. From *A Star Is Born* (1954) © 1954 (Renewed) Harwin Music Corp. and New World Music Company (Ltd.).[23]

INDEX OF TITLES